At War in the Pacific

# At War in the Pacific

*Personal Accounts of
World War II Navy and
Marine Corps Officers*

Bruce M. Petty

McFarland & Company, Inc., Publishers
*Jefferson, North Carolina, and London*

LIBRARY OF CONGRESS CATALOGUING-IN-PUBLICATION DATA

Petty, Bruce M., 1945–
   At war in the Pacific : personal accounts of World War II Navy
and Marine Corps officers / Bruce M. Petty.
     p.    cm.
   Includes bibliographical references and index.

   **ISBN 0-7864-2373-0** (softcover : 50# alkaline paper) ∞

   1. World War, 1939–1945—Campaigns—Pacific Area.   2. World
War, 1939–1945—Naval operations, American.   3. World War, 1939–
1945—Personal narratives, American.   4. United States. Navy—
Officers—Biography.   5. United States. Marine Corps—Officers—
Biography.   6. Oral history.   I. Title.
D767.P475   2006
940.54'59730922—dc22                          2005027664

British Library cataloguing data are available

On the cover: Navy fighter ace Alex Vraciu climbing out of his F6F Hellcat

Manufactured in the United States of America

*McFarland & Company, Inc., Publishers*
  *Box 611, Jefferson, North Carolina 28640*
   *www.mcfarlandpub.com*

For my children,
Anne-Marie, Beatrice Jeanne, and Faris Marcel

# Acknowledgments

As with my other books, I would like to thank the many hundreds of people who shared their stories with me. And as is the case so often in a work like this, I was not able to use all of the stories these people contributed even though I learned much from every person I talked to.

More than anybody else I would like to thank my wife, Dr. Daniele Lonchamp-Petty, who, as a wife, mother, and only breadwinner in the family, made it emotionally and financially possible for me to research and write this book.

Again too, I would like to thank my dear and ever-faithful friend Dr. Beret E. Strong, for always being there as my unofficial editor, confidant, and confidence builder.

Below are other people who contributed to my efforts to put this book together. I hope I didn't forget anybody: Dr. Bill Lee of Saint Maries University in Moraga, California, Paul Stillwell, Ann Hessinger; Mark Gatlin, Capt. Tim Wooldridge USN-Ret.; Marybeth Lysons Filice; Maria Theresita "Thet" Nebre; Joseph Abado; Joven S. Ramirez, Jr.; Michael B. Reaso; Eugene Zarsuela; and Arnel Garcia. Also, Col. Joseph Alexander, USMC-Ret.; Bill Winnekins; Dale Barker; Mike Lyga; Capt. William Van Dusen, USN-Ret.; Peter Flahavin of Melbourne, Australia; Elaine and Harry Dallas; Bill Mozinga, USN-Ret.; Harris Martin; Hill Goodspeed of the Natrional Museum of Naval Aviation; and Tiny Clarkson, Jim Talbert, and John Cummer of the LCI Association.

# Table of Contents

*Acknowledgments*                                                vii

*Preface*                                                         1

*Timeline of the War in the Pacific*                             7

*Glossary of Terms*                                             11

Senior Officer Aboard the USS *Nevada*, BB-36, Pearl
    Harbor, 7 December 1941—*Rear Admiral Francis
    Thomas, USN (Ret.)*                      15

From the USS *Honolulu* to Senior Aviator of Scouting
    Squadron Ringbolt—*Capt. Larry Pierce, USN (Ret.)*   25

Marine Corps Fighter Pilot—*Lt. Col. H.A.P. Langstaff,
    USMC (Ret.)*                             34

Carrier Air Group Sixteen, USS *Lexington*, CV-16—
    *Lt. Cmdr. James Arquette, USN (Ret.)*   46

Navy Fighter Ace—*Cmdr. Alexander Vraciu, USN (Ret.)*          54

Landing Signal Officer, USS *Chenango*, CVE-28—
    *Cmdr. Frank Malinasky, USN (Ret.)*      71

Sailor/Marine/Fighter Pilot—*Capt. Bernard W. Peterson,
    USMCR (Ret.)*                            78

Aboard the USS *Bailey*, DD-492—*Stanley M. Hogshead*          89

USS *Arizona* Survivor—*Joseph K. Langdell*                    96

HMAS *Canberra* and the Battle of Saveo Island—*Lt. Cmdr.
MacKenzie Jesse Gregory, Royal Australian Navy (Ret.)*    100

"The *Helena* Doesn't Answer"—*Cmdr. Bill Barnett,
USN (Ret.)*    108

Aboard the USS *Zane*, DMS-14—*Capt. Joseph B. Drachnik,
USN (Ret.)*    114

Aboard the USS *Long*, DMS-12—*Benjamin F. Cator*    124

Aboard the USS *Charles Carroll*, APA-28—*Lt. Kenneth
Barden, USNR (Ret.)*    132

USS *LCI (L)-981*—*John F. Harrington*    139

My Flight with Lt. Arthur G. Elder—*Bernard Isaacs*    153

The Mustanger—*Lt. Cmdr. Warren Decious,
USN (Ret.)*    157

The Rescuers—*Capt. William C. Meyer, USN (Ret.)*    163

Japanese-Language Officer—*Willard H. Elsbree*    171

Navy Weatherman—*Dr. Gaylord Whitlock*    178

Master Rigger, Mare Island Naval Shipyard—*Cmdr.
Eddie Martinez, USNR (Ret.)*    184

*Selected Bibliography*    191
*Index*    193

# Preface

Over sixteen million Americans served in the U.S. military during World War II. Close to three million Americans served in the Pacific. Before Pearl Harbor, the United States looked to graduates of the nation's naval academy to fill the nation's need for qualified naval officers. However, even before World War II the navy sought to supplement the numbers coming out of the naval academy by introducing the Naval Reserve Officer Training Program at a number of universities in 1926. There were also other innovative training programs which came later, such as the Civilian Pilot Training Program, Naval Aviation Cadet Program, and what were later called the various "V" programs. (See the abbreviated Timeline beginning on page 7 for dates.)

Before the United States started its slow and inadequate military buildup prior to the Japanese attack on Pearl Harbor, advancement for both enlisted personnel and officers was painfully slow. Some officers, including Academy graduates, elected to leave the service in favor of more lucrative prospects in the private sector, although the high unemployment rate during the Depression made staying in the navy an easy choice for many. Some naval officers, however, remained in the Naval Reserves, and were recalled either just before or right after the U.S. entry into the war. Even some naval officers who had left the service for medical reasons found themselves recalled to active duty.

An example of one of the above situations is Adm. Joseph M. Reeves. Reeves was born in 1872 and was a graduate of the U.S. Naval Academy. He was one of the pioneers of naval aviation as well as aircraft carrier development before World War II. He retired in 1936, but was recalled

1

to active duty in 1940, and spent most of the war as the Navy Department's Liaison Officer for Lend-Lease.

Reservists were being called to active duty even before the Japanese attack on Pearl Harbor, and after Pearl Harbor all branches of the military service became dependent on officers rushed through programs, some lasting not much longer than the enlisted men's boot camp—the so-called Ninety-Day Wonders. In addition, there were career enlisted men who worked their way up through the ranks to earn commissions. They were known then, and still are today, as "mustangers."

World War II was also a watershed for minorities. The V-12 program ushered in the first black Americans to be commissioned in the history of the U.S. Navy. Bernard Isaacs was a mentor to one of them before going on to become an officer himself—a Ninety-Day Wonder. His story appears in this book.

The U.S. Navy before World War II was a fraction of what it was by war's end. There were very few aircraft carriers. The first one, converted from a collier, was not commissioned until the 1920s. Most U.S. battleships had been built before or during World War I, as were so many U.S. submarines, destroyers, and cruisers. Even auxiliary ships were in short supply. But once the United States found itself at war, everything from luxury passenger liners, commercial oil tankers, and even commercial fishing boats were leased or bought outright by the navy and converted to military use. The navy, as well as the nation as a whole, displayed a remarkable flexibility of mind and purpose once total war engulfed it.

From December 1941 through all of 1943, the U.S. and its allies were barely able to stay afloat, literally and figuratively, in the Pacific. The United States suffered some of its worst naval defeats in history during the first eighteen months of the war. Ship after ship and battle after battle were lost in the waters around the Solomon Islands. The U.S. and Australia lost four cruisers in a matter of minutes at the Battle of Savo Island in August 1942, and in the overall battle for Guadalcanal, the U.S. Navy lost more men than the marines did.

There were many naval firsts in the war in the Pacific. The Battle of the Coral Sea in May 1942 was the first sea battle fought between aircraft carriers. Both sides lost ships, but the Japanese advance south towards Australia was stopped.

The Battle of Midway, again between aircraft carriers, was fought just a month later and resulted in an unquestionable victory for the United

States, although the U.S. lost the wounded *Yorktown*, which had been hurriedly patched up after the Battle of the Coral Sea. The Japanese, however, lost four of their valuable carriers as well as some of their finest and hard-to-replace navy pilots. The United States was still losing ships faster than they could be replaced, but U.S. industrial might and the determination of the entire nation would soon turn that around.

As the war moved into 1943, more ships were being built to fill the void left by a nation unprepared for war before December 1941. The older U.S. submarines—some going back as far as World War I—were being replaced by the newer "fleet boats." Torpedo problems that had hindered the navy's ability to sink enemy ships were slowly—too slowly—being resolved. The handful of carriers available to fight the war in the Pacific would be replaced and augmented with more than a hundred such vessels by war's end. New classes of ships, such as the destroyer escort, patrol craft, and a variety of amphibious warfare craft, were brought on line to fill the need for more ships needed *now*. They were needed for a war, the likes of which had never been fought before.

Although most Americans view the war in the Pacific as having been primarily between the two main adversaries, the Americans and the Japanese, the U.S. did have allies in the Asia/Pacific theaters, just as in Europe. Australian troops did much of the fighting and dying in the southern command under Gen. Douglas MacArthur, but received little recognition from MacArthur in his plethora of press releases. Nor do Americans get much information about the role of Allied sailors and soldiers in the war from histories written by Americans. Gen. MacArthur's propensity to brush over or ignore the presence and sacrifice of Her Majesty's forces under his command still rankles many Australian and New Zealand veterans, as I have discovered.

During the early days of the war in the Pacific, it was the British and Dutch and their colonial allies who suffered greatly under the advance of Japanese forces, as did U.S. forces in Hawaii, the Philippines and on Guam. Australian and a few British ships and aircraft squadrons also supplemented the meager U.S. forces in the early days of war when the main objective was stopping the lightning advances of Imperial Japanese forces.

Australian and New Zealand ships, especially, were incorporated into U.S. fleet and task force formations. The Australian ship HMAS *Canberra* was one of them and was also one of four Allied cruisers sunk by the Japanese at the Battle of Savo Island in the Solomons in August 1942. McKenzie Gregory of the Royal Australian Navy was a young naval officer aboard HMAS *Canberra* at the time and survived the sinking to tell his story in this book.

My mother, my father, and one uncle served in the U.S. Navy during World War II. A generation later, I too served in the Pacific as a young petty officer aboard the USS *Yorktown* during the Vietnam War. I crossed the Pacific on five different occasions and visited many of the sites where great battles took place and men died. And even though I was involved in one war, for some reason the one that was fought before mine fascinated me more. After all, it was the biggest human event of the twentieth century. It compressed life for millions of people who were witness to it, and for many of them everything they did after the war seemed mundane and secondary.

The men and women of my parents' generation, for the most part, were ordinary people who lived extraordinary lives during World War II. As one of my history professors, who fought as a foot soldier in Italy during World War II, told me many years ago, "It was a great experience if you lived through it."

Having interviewed hundreds of World War II veterans and their families for previous works, I was able to fall back on references to find former naval officers to interview for this book. However, as I discovered when I was researching my first book, *Saipan: Oral Histories of the Pacific War*, the Internet is a valuable and time-saving source. There are any number of World War II Internet sites with bulletin boards where veterans and their families can post messages in an effort to locate old shipmates, or perhaps find somebody who might have information on a father or grandfather who has passed away. However, in this case, instead of finding an old shipmate, they found me.

For this particular book, I also discovered the Pearl Harbor Survivors Association and its many regional chapters. Those in the greater San Francisco Bay area and Sacramento area of California proved to be the most fruitful, being that they were both within close driving distance from where we lived at the time.

In addition, I discovered that most ships, some as small as destroyer escorts, have associations that sponsor newsletters and have regular reunions. Even the smallest of seagoing vessels such as LCIs have a large and active association through which I was able to contact veterans willing to tell their stories. And living in the Fairfield-Vacaville area of California while researching this book, I was happy to discover a good number of World War II navy veterans within a few minutes' drive of where we lived.

In this introduction and the abbreviated timeline I have tried to give an overview of World War II in the Pacific to those who might be first-time readers on the subject. But the real story of this war—any war, as far as I'm concerned—is that of the men and women, once young, who served in that war, and I shall leave its telling to them.

# Timeline of the
# War in the Pacific

Events that affected the men and women who served in the U.S. Navy in the Pacific during World War II.

1922—Naval Disarmament Treaty signed by U.S., Britain, and Japan.

1925—Naval Reserve Officer Training Corps established.

1927—The carrier *Lexington* is commissioned.

1929—The stock market crashes, throwing millions of people out of work.

1933—Franklin D. Roosevelt is elected president of the United States. Congress is prodded into appropriating funds for a long-neglected military. Construction of two more carriers—*Yorktown* and *Enterprise*—are authorized.

1934—Funding for two more carriers—*Hornet* and *Wasp*—are authorized.

1935—Navy Aviation Cadet (V-5) Program inaugurated.

1939—CPTP (Civilian Pilot Training Program) started under FDR's New Deal.

1941 *(Dec.)*—Japanese attack Pearl Harbor and other U.S bases in the Philippines and Guam, as well as Dutch and British colonial possessions in Southeast Asia. The U.S. Congress votes an additional $10.1

billion post–Pearl Harbor to aid the war effort. Adm. Ernest King is named commander in chief of the U.S. fleet; later he will be named chief of naval operations, replacing Adm. Harold R. Stark. U.S. troops start arriving in Australia. Adm. Chester Nimitz named to take command of the Pacific Fleet, headquartered at Pearl Harbor. U.S submarines ordered to commence unrestricted attacks against Japanese shipping.

**1942 (Jan./Feb.)**—U.S. carriers begin the first of a series of raids against Japanese islands in the Central Pacific. Singapore falls to Japanese forces.

**(March/April)**—The oil fields of the Dutch East Indies fall to Japanese forces. U.S. Army B-25s launched from deck of the carrier *Hornet* bomb Japan.

**(May)**—Battle of the Coral Sea: The first carrier-against-carrier battle in history. Corregidor, in the Philippines, finally surrenders.

**(June)**—The Battle of Midway: The second carrier-against-carrier battle in history, and the first decisive victory for the United States in the war against Japan, with Japan losing four carriers, the U.S. one (*Yorktown*). The U.S. Naval Academy graduates its first three-year class. The navy's Japanese Language School is moved from Berkeley, California, to the University of Colorado at Boulder.

**(Aug.)**—The Battle of Guadalcanal begins: the first in a long line of counteroffensives begun by U.S. forces against Imperial Japan. Numerous naval battles are fought in offshore waters, resulting in the loss of more sailors than marines by the time the battle is over. Gen. MacArthur begins his long march across Papua New Guinea on his way back to the Philippines.

**(Sept.)**—The carrier *Wasp* sunk by Japanese submarine.

**(Oct.)**—Adm. Halsey made Allied commander in the South Pacific. Carrier *Hornet* is lost in Battle of Santa Cruz Islands.

**(Nov.)**—Cruiser *Juneau* is lost to multiple torpedo hits from Japanese submarine with loss of most of its crew, including the five Sullivan brothers.

**1943 (Feb.)**—Japanese evacuate troops from Guadalcanal.

**(April)**—Adm. Isoroku Yamamoto, architect of Japan's war with the U.S., is shot down and killed with the help of U.S. code breakers.

*(July)*—Navy V-12 program instituted.

*(Nov.)*—Adm. Nimitz launches the Central Pacific offensive with marine and army amphibious landings in the Gilbert Islands (Tarawa/ Makin). One of many new escort carriers, *Liscome Bay*, torpedoed by Japanese submarine with the loss of more than six hundred officers and men.

1943—By the middle of 1943, U.S. submarines start making headway in their effort to sink Japanese shipping, with more submarines coming on line (67 since Pearl Harbor) and problems with defective torpedoes being resolved. Japan goes on the defensive. By war's end, many will have died from disease and starvation. Japan is also losing more ships than can be replaced, especially merchant ships. The U.S. is building more ships than are being lost (31 new carriers since Pearl Harbor). The tide is turning.

1944 *(Jan.)*—U.S. Marines and army troops make amphibious landings in Marshall Islands on the next step to taking the war home to Japan. U.S. Navy ships and airplanes dominate Pacific waters, sinking on average fifty Japanese ships a month.

*(May)*—The U.S. destroyer escort *England* sinks six Japanese submarines in twelve days, thanks to U.S. code breakers.

*(June–July)*—The Mariana Islands, Japan's outer ring of defense, is broken with landings on Saipan, Tinian, and Guam. Prime Minister Hideki Tojo and his entire cabinet resign in Tokyo. First Battle of the Philippines Sea—"The Great Marianas Turkey Shoot"—delivers another decisive blow against Japan's Imperial Navy. U.S. submarines unknowingly kill over 4,000 Allied POWs being transported to Japan by ship.

*(Oct.)*—MacArthur's forces make first landings in the Philippines at Leyte. Several major naval battles are fought, with the Japanese making the first organized use of kamikazes to stop Allied advances. Escort carriers *Suwanee* and *Santee* hit by kamikazes within minutes of each other with tremendous loss of life. Japanese super battleship *Musashi* sunk by U.S. carrier aircraft. Japanese make first use of *kaiten*, human torpedoes, sinking the U.S. oiler *Mississinewa* at Ulithi Atoll.

*(Nov.)*—First B-29 raids against the Japanese home islands are launched from bases in the Marianas. (The very first were launched from bases in China.)

*(Dec.)*—U.S. submarines are running out of Japanese ships to sink.

**1945** *(Feb.)*—U.S. Marines assault and take the island of Iwo Jima. The bloodiest fight in Marine Corps history.

*(Apr.)*—Okinawa, the last major battle of World War II, and the bloodiest for U.S. forces in the Pacific. The U.S. Navy suffers 10,000 casualties and hundreds of ships sunk or damaged, mostly from aerial attack by kamikazes. President Roosevelt dies on April 12. Hitler commits suicide on April 30.

*(Aug.)*—The USS *Indianapolis,* after delivering parts of the first atomic bomb to the island of Tinian in the Marianas, is torpedoed and sunk by a Japanese submarine. Japan surrenders following the dropping of two atomic bombs. The war is over but thousands of Japanese stranded throughout the Pacific and Asia die of disease and starvation before they can be repatriated. Others refuse to surrender for years, even decades.

*(Dec.)*—Last organized Japanese resistance on Saipan ends. (The last Japanese holdout on Guam will not be captured until the 1970s.)

# Glossary of Terms

ABSD—auxiliary floating dry dock

AH—hospital ship

AKA—attack cargo ship

AO—fleet oiler

APA—attack transport

APD—high-speed destroyer transport

AS—submarine tender

ATF—fleet tug

ATR—auxiliary tug, rescue

A.W.O.L.—absent without leave

BB—battleship

CA—heavy cruiser

CAP—combat air patrol (defensive)

CINCPAC—Commander in Chief, Pacific Fleet

CL—light cruiser

CO—commanding officer

CPTP—Civilian Pilot Training Program (changed to War Training Service after Pearl Harbor).

CV—attack aircraft carrier

CVE—escort carrier (smaller than a CV)

DD—destroyer

DE—destroyer escort

DesRon—destroyer squadron

DMS—fast minesweeper, mostly converted old four-stack destroyers

fleet boat—U.S. submarine type. Replaced smaller, older models from World War I and post–World War I.

hedgehogs—a throw-ahead explosive device used against submarines.

JICPOA—Joint Intelligence Center Pacific Ocean Area.

*kaiten*—manned suicide torpedo (Japanese)

11

**knots**—a nautical mile, equal to 1.15 land miles.

**LCI**—landing craft infantry

**LCI(G)**—landing craft, infantry converted to a gun ship

**LCI(L)**—landing craft, infantry (large)

**LCI(R)**—landing craft, infantry converted to launch rockets

**LCM**—landing craft, medium

**LCP**—landing craft, personnel

**LCT**—landing craft, tank

**LCVP**—landing craft, vehicle and personnel

**LSD**—landing ship, dock

**LSO**—landing signal officer

**LST**—landing ship, tank

**LVT**—amphibious tractors

**MCAS**—Marine Corps Air Station

**MTB** or **PT**—motor torpedo boats

**NAS**—naval air station

**NAVTRASCH**—Naval Training School

**Ninety-Day Wonder**—A reserve officer rushed through three months of training. Sometimes, but not always a college graduate.

**NROTC**—Naval Reserve Officer Training Corps

**PC**—patrol craft

**petty officers**—enlisted ratings

**PGM**—submarine chaser (patrol craft) converted to a gunboat

**POW**—prisoner of war

**radar picket**—usually a destroyer or destroyer escort. Used primarily as an early warning system against kamikazes.

**Ret.**—retired

**S-Boat**—pre–World War II submarine, later replaced by newer, bigger fleet boats

**"slot"**—The channel of water running northwest and southeast in the Solomon Islands where most of the naval activity took place during the struggle for control of these islands.

**TF**—task force

**TG**—task group

**tin can**—destroyer

**UDT**—underwater demolition (frogmen)

**USN**—United States Navy

**USNR**—United States Naval Reserve

**vector**—A magnetic heading, used to direct planes to a potential target

**VF**—navy fighter squadron

**VMF**—marine corps fighter squadron

**VPB**—navy patrol bombing squadron

WAC—Women's Army Corps

WAVE—female members of the U.S. Navy

YO—small oiler

YP—yard patrol craft

## U.S. Navy Ranks

Adm.—admiral

Capt.—captain

Cmdr.—commander

Ens.—ensign

Lt.—lieutenant

Lt. Cmdr.—lieutenant commander

Lt. (jg)—lieutenant junior grade

R. Adm.—rear admiral

V. Adm.—vice admiral

W.O.—warrant officer

## U.S. Naval Aircraft

F4F—Wildcat, fighter

F4U—Corsair, fighter flown mostly by the Marine Corps

F6F—Hellcat, fighter

PBM Mariner—Seaplane built by Martin Aircraft Company

PBY—Catalina seaplane used mostly for reconnaissance; also carried bombs

SOC—floatplane, flown for the most part off cruisers and battleships

TBM and TBF—torpedo planes (Grumman/Gen. Motors)

# Senior Officer Aboard the USS *Nevada*, BB-36, Pearl Harbor, 7 December 1941

## REAR ADMIRAL FRANCIS THOMAS, USN (RET.)

*Rear Admiral Thomas entered the U.S. Naval Academy at the age of sixteen and graduated in the class of 1925. He served on active duty with the U.S. Navy until 1929. He then worked as a civilian for a steel company, but later joined the Naval Reserves. He was recalled to active duty in February 1941 and distinguished himself during the attack on Pearl Harbor by getting the USS* Nevada *underway in response to orders to leave the harbor. After World War II, he was eventually allowed to return to civilian life and his job with the steel company. After retirement, he and his wife served for several years with the Peace Corps in the Fiji Islands. As I write this, Rear Admiral Thomas, USNR (Ret.), is an active ninety-five-year-old. I spoke with him at his son's home in Columbia, Missouri, after he had arrived back there from a circuitous drive through parts of the western U.S.*

I have always been a man of peace rather than a man of war, but I kept finding myself in situations where I didn't want to be. I didn't want to be at Pearl Harbor, for example. But as a damage control officer I wanted to keep our ship fighting after the Japanese attacked.

Going back a ways, I graduated from the Naval Academy in 1925, I

**Rear Admiral Francis Thomas. Photograph taken sometime in 1941 when he was still a lieutenant commander.**

served on a new cruiser, the USS *Richmond*. I had duty in the Pacific, the Atlantic, and the Asiatic stations in China and the Philippines. That was before I decided I wanted to be an aviator, and that's when the navy sent me to Pensacola, Florida. After a short time there, they got rid of me because I damaged one of their planes while landing. I felt bad about that, but I also felt it wasn't my fault. After that, the navy sent me to Washington, to the Naval Research Laboratory, and put me on board a small ship called *Eagle #58*. I was a research officer on her, and we were developing what is now known as sonar. We would go out while submarines ran around below us, and we would try and pick them up.

I was beginning to wonder why I was in the navy, and it was about that time that the great statesmen of the world sat down and signed the Kellogg-Briand Pact, outlawing war as an instrument of national policy. All nations agreed to resolve all disputes and conflicts, whatever their nature or origin, by peaceful means. That meant to me that I didn't need to stay in the navy anymore since there would be no use for one. So I resigned and went to work for a steel company. I was walking along the street one day and a friend drove by and said, "How come you're out of the navy?" I said, "Well, because I'm working for a steel company." Then he said, "Come on down and join the Naval Reserves. We have a sub chaser down on the Niagara River, and we have a wonderful time down there." So I went down there and joined the Naval Reserves. That was in Niagara Falls, New York. We met once a week and had drills.

Eventually, the steel company moved me to Cleveland and I became the commanding officer of the Naval Reserve unit in Cleveland, Ohio. I had a pretty good job with the steel company by that time, and I had an office on the sixteenth floor of the Republic Building in downtown Cleveland. One December, I was looking out over Lake Erie at a terrific winter storm. The waves were dashing up over the break wall, and I was patting myself on the back, thinking, "Boy, am I glad I'm on dry land." Then the phone rang, and a friend of mine in Washington said I was being recalled to active duty. I said, "You can't do that! The steel company can't get along without me." He said, "We'll see about that."

Two months later I was in San Diego, and walked aboard an old World War I destroyer, USS *Kennison*, DD-158, as the executive officer and navigator. The officer I was relieving was in a hurry because he had to catch another ship, which was leaving in ten minutes. However, before he left he took me down to meet the captain, and the captain—I won't use the words he used—said, "What are you doing here?" As it turned out, he was an old friend of mine. I had introduced him to the gal he married, and they were still happily married.

I called up my wife and told her I was all set up: "You stay in Cleveland. I'll make out all right." And on the next train from Cleveland, there she was. Well, we enjoyed it there. We had a place in Coronado, across the bay from San Diego.

Then, four months later, orders came through detaching me and sending me out to Pearl Harbor to USS *Nevada*. There was an admiral out there by the name of Richardson who objected to keeping the fleet in Pearl Harbor. He went back to Washington and told President Roosevelt It would be better to put it on the West Coast. The next thing he knew he was replaced by Admiral Kimmel, and Richardson was sent to some desk job.

*Nevada* was an old battleship and wasn't in all that good a condition, I didn't think. They really didn't have a job for me, but I had an old friend on board from my early cruiser days who was the damage control officer. So I was given to him as his assistant. I went around the ship and tried to make myself busy, and I found that things weren't as they should be. After a while the other top officers realized I was an academy man and not just a reserve officer out of Notre Dame or someplace, so they started accepting me. I was then allowed to take "command" watches, with the captain's approval.

It came along about November 1941, when the captain started getting messages to look out when at sea—there might be some Jap submarines out there. So while at sea we would be on the alert. Whenever we got back to Pearl Harbor we felt safe because everybody in the navy knew you couldn't torpedo a battleship in Pearl Harbor. The water was too shallow and the distance from where a torpedo could be dropped was too short. But the Japanese had been working on this problem for about five or six years, and they had developed some torpedoes that would stay just below the surface and pick up speed in a short distance.

We came into port on 5 December 1941, after being out at sea for about ten days on a training cruise. That evening I went on shore leave and walked around the Japanese section of Honolulu and I could almost sense that something was about to happen, but I didn't know what it was.

The Saturday before the Japanese attacked Pearl Harbor, which was 6 December, after the captain's inspection, all the senior officers, except me, went ashore. The gunnery officer, a fellow named Arvon J. Robertson—we all called him Robby—had the duty. His main job that afternoon was to take all of the 14-inch projectiles and put them in a lighter alongside of the ship. By that afternoon, he had it all off the ship so that we didn't have any main battery ammunition on board. On the following Monday, another lighter was to come down with some more up-to-date main battery ammunition, and we would put it aboard. Nobody thought much about all this ammo sitting alongside of us till Monday morning.

That evening after the movie, Robby asked me if I would take his duty. I said, "Robby, I don't want to do that. I'm planning to go to church tomorrow morning in Honolulu." "Oh," he said. "That's no problem whatsoever. I'll be on the dock at eight o'clock in the morning. Just have a boat come over and get me, and you can leave the ship around

9:00 A.M., or whatever." I wasn't very fond of Robby anyhow, but I couldn't think of any good reason not to take his duty, so I agreed. I was now the senior officer on board.

It was a beautiful morning, 7 December 1941. I was up around about six o'clock in the morning. I went around and saw the officer of the deck and the junior officer of the deck. Then I went down and had breakfast in the wardroom. The wardroom extended the entire width of the ship, with portholes on the port side and the starboard side. I was the only officer in there that morning. All of the other senior officers were ashore.

After breakfast, I was sitting there reading the newspaper when I heard what I thought was some riveting going on in the navy yard. Actually, it was the Japanese strafing Hickam Field. I looked out one of the portholes on the port side and looked toward Hickam Field but couldn't see anything. So then I walked over to the starboard side and looked out a porthole. I saw a plane fly by at the level of the porthole—pretty low. I looked at it and saw the red balls on the wings. At first I thought the Army Air Force had painted up some of their planes to look like Japanese. Then I looked off toward Ford Island and saw a tank with aviation gasoline in it, and it was throwing up flames like a torch. It was about then that the officer of the deck called the alarm, "All hands, man your battle stations!" I dashed back to where he was, back by the number three turret. When I got there, there was a young officer whose battle station was the number three turret. Well, I knew that turret wasn't going to be of any use, so I had him relieve the O.O.D. [Officer of the Day], an ensign by the name of Joe Taussig. His father was Admiral Taussig that I had known in cruisers back in the twenties. I sent young Taussig up to his battle station, an antiaircraft director near the bridge, and as soon as he got up there a bomb fragment took his leg off.

My battle station was down in what could be called the bowels of the ship, down below the third deck in a little compartment called central station. It had all the equipment to operate the ship from. It was put there when the ship was built, figuring that if the ship's bridge and all the control stations topside were shot away you could operate the ship from central station. Down there, we had everything we had on the bridge, including phone connections to every part of the ship, and that's the place where the damage control headquarters was. By the time I got there everybody was reporting that things were as they should be, and our antiaircraft batteries were firing at the Jap planes.

**USS *Nevada*, BB-36, on 7 December 1941, after it had been damaged by bombs dropped from Japanese aircraft attacking Pearl Harbor.**

After the war I read an article in *Naval Proceedings* written by a Japanese naval aviator, and I would meet him in 1948 at a church in Berea, Ohio. His name was Mitsuo Fuchida. He was from one of the Japanese carriers, and he flew a special plane that day. It had yellow and black stripes painted on it. That was to show that he was the head man of the operation that day.

One hundred eighty Japanese planes came in at us in that first wave. First they hit the air fields at Hickam and Ford Island. Then they went after the battleships, which is rather peculiar, looking back now. I guess they had the same idea as some of our old timers, that the battleships were important.

Fuchida was in a high-level dive-bomber. He came down with his group for the battleships. Fuchida was the lead plane. He was going to get the *Nevada*. The next plane was going to get the *Arizona*, and so on. Just as he got to where he was going to drop his bomb on the *Nevada*, a cloud got in his way, so he circled around. When he tried to drop his bomb on the *Nevada* the second time something else happened. A great ball of flame shot up from the *Arizona* and diverted him.

Our ship was only about one hundred feet astern of the *Arizona*. I didn't know about the *Arizona* getting hit. If I had been topside I would have seen it. Then I received a report that we had taken a torpedo hit port side, forward. It did a lot of damage, and water started flooding in, and the ship started listing to port. We had what they call "blister tanks," and by counter flooding the starboard blister tanks we got the ship back up on an even keel.

Shortly after that we got a couple of bomb hits from high-level bombers. One of them came down through the bridge and wiped out practically the whole bridge. Meanwhile, a message went out from the harbor control tower for all ships to clear the harbor.

I left central station and climbed up to the armored conning tower, holding all the people we needed to get underway. I looked forward and could see the *Arizona* was ablaze. There didn't seem to be any part of it that wasn't burning. I looked a little further ahead and saw the bottom of the *Oklahoma*. Now, the *Oklahoma* had taken more torpedo hits than any of the other ships, and all of the hits were on the port side. It started listing, then turned over, trapping many people inside. The ones who were topside kept climbing over the bottom.

The ship usually got underway in peacetime with tugs forward and tugs aft. We didn't have any tugs, but we did have a little steam up, so I gave orders to move out. We managed to sail down the port side of the *Arizona*. We got by her and sailed down the channel. We weren't going very fast and hadn't reached the mouth of the harbor when we received a signal from the control tower, "Do not! Repeat, do not leave the harbor!" We couldn't leave and we couldn't go back, so what were we to do?

I decided to get out of the way of any other ships and anchor at one side of the channel. Now, it was almost an hour after the first wave of Jap planes arrived, and they started back to their ships. As they started back, a second wave came in. The second wave had 171 planes, but none of them were torpedo bombers. As we made up our minds that we were going to anchor, the Jap dive bombers came after us because they saw us heading for the entrance to the harbor. We were the only battleship underway, and they had orders to get the battleships. Only three bombs hit us. I think the reason was because we had stopped our engines and had turned our head to port to come to anchor. We did get hit, but all the hits were in the bow, forward of the turrets. That indicated to me that by my slowing us down we had thrown off their aim, and many of the other bombs missed but exploded all around us.

Unfortunately, we had sent an anchoring party forward to get ready to let the anchor go. From the conning tower we didn't have any communication with them, and we couldn't see over the top of the turrets down to where they were, so Chief Boatswain E.J. Hill, who was in charge of the topside repair party, sent his assistant back around the turret to stand right under the conning tower, and I was to tell them when to let go the anchor. They were all ready to do that when these bomb hits came. One of them dropped right in the middle of them. It penetrated down through three or four decks until it hit the armored deck and bounced back up before it exploded. All of the people on the forward part of the ship were killed.

We also had a repair party just below the armored deck where the bomb hit, and the way they knew there was a bomb hit was because the overhead came down about three or four inches and bounced back up. By that time the ship was aground. I got credit afterwards for running the ship aground. As far as I know I'm the only naval officer who ever got a medal for running a battleship aground. They gave me the Navy Cross for which I don't see any good reason, but I accepted it.

Now that we were run aground we weren't going anywhere and we had a fire in the forward part of the ship, so I went to get a repair party and put some of those fires out. That was my job anyhow. As I went back aft to find somebody I met the captain of the ship, Capt. F. W. Scanland. He had come back aboard. I reported to him and gave charge of the ship back to him. However, I didn't give it back to him as good as when he left it.

The ship had a lot of damage, but all the engineering departments, with the exception of one boiler, were in relative good shape. The only thing is we couldn't get any firemain pressure forward to where the bombs hit. We couldn't put the fires out, so we got a couple of tugboats alongside and started getting some water from them. I went below and saw there was some flooding, so we tried to keep it from working aft. Meanwhile the other officers and men had returned to the ship and we went to work trying to stop the flooding. This went on for about twenty-four hours. I remember going below; it was about three in the morning and I was soaking wet. Somebody had a radio down there and I heard President Roosevelt addressing Congress or somebody. He was saying we

were in a state of war. I
agreed with him on that.

Our dentist on board
was woken up by a book
falling on his head. The
book fell on his head when
the torpedo struck our ship.
After all the dust had settled and the smoke had
cleared away, he was the
one who had to go around
and inspect all the dead
and try to identify them by
their dental records.

Mr. Fuchida stayed
around and tried to assess
the damage, but he couldn't
see too much because of
the smoke coming from
the *Arizona*. He had been
hanging around the area for

**Rear Admiral Francis Thomas, winner of the
Navy Cross for his actions in saving *Nevada*
during the attack on Pearl Harbor. Photograph taken Memorial Day, 1999.**

about one hour and finally went back to his carrier and reported what
damage he had seen to Admiral Nagomo. Fuchida recommended that he
send in another strike, but Nagomo said, "How are our planes going to
see what to strike with all that smoke up there? Besides, we don't know
where their carriers are." Nagomo then retired to the north and headed
for Japan. He was later criticized for not following Fuchida's recommen-
dations.

Practically all the people were taken off the *Nevada*. I remained with
a skeleton crew, and was one of those in charge of refloating the ship.
Every compartment on the ship up to the main deck, and including part
of the main deck, was flooded. The *Nevada* was a dead ship! We brought
pumps on board and refloated her and towed her to a dry dock where
USS *Pennsylvania* had been.

Admiral Nimitz came aboard and started awarding medals to a number of people who had been there during the attack and who had reacted
favorably. As far as I was concerned, everybody who was there should
have gotten medals. Somehow or other, I was awarded the Navy Cross,

but I didn't get the medal. The reason for that is rather strange. At the Great Lakes Naval Station there was a Naval Reserve officer by the name of Francis J. Thomas, and the Navy Department sent the Navy Cross to the Commandant of the Fourth Naval District at Great Lakes, with instructions to award Lt. Commander Francis J. Thomas the Navy Cross.

You can imagine what happened. They were trying to figure out why this guy was being awarded for heroism while conducting classes at the Great Lakes Naval Training Station. Well, the medal was sent to Admiral Nimitz, and by that time we had got the ship going again and had taken her back to Puget Sound Navy Yard, just across from Seattle. We were busy making a new ship out of her, and this admiral over there in Seattle got this medal. He was told to make a big deal out of it, so they stopped all the work on the ship and I was awarded the Navy Cross there.

After the war was over I went back to work for the steel company. One day I was walking by a Methodist church in Berea, Ohio, and saw a sign that said a Japanese man by the name of Mitsuo Fuchida was giving a talk there that evening. I went in to hear what he had to say. After the war he became a Christian convert and preacher in Japan. So here he was preaching about his conversion story at churches all around America. I was sitting in the back of the church listening to him. After the service was over people went up and talked to him. I shook his hand and complimented him on being a Christian. I didn't tell him I was at Pearl Harbor. I didn't have any friendly feeling towards him and never had any contact with him after that.

# From the USS *Honolulu* to Senior Aviator of Scouting Squadron Ringbolt

## CAPT. LARRY PIERCE, USN (RET.)

*Capt. Larry Pierce was born in Marked Tree, Arkansas, in 1917. His father had served briefly as an enlisted man in the U.S. Navy during the Spanish-American War, and his older brother, Ransom, entered the U.S. Naval Academy as a plebe in the summer of 1927. Capt. Pierce followed in his brother's footsteps seven years later and graduated from the Academy in 1938. Prior to his acceptance to naval flight training in Pensacola, Florida, he served as a young ensign aboard the cruiser USS* Chester *and destroyer USS* Buck. *As an aviator, he flew SOC-float planes, first off the USS* Honolulu, *a light cruiser, then as commanding officer of Scouting Squadron "Ringbolt," the code name for the area on Florida Island where his squadron of ten float planes flew out of in the Solomon Islands. After Guadalcanal had been secured and his squadron relieved, Captain Pierce returned to the United States and trained in a variety of fighter aircraft, became carrier qualified, and ended the war as squadron commander of VF-36 aboard the USS* Siboney. *After World War II, Captain Pierce served as air officer aboard carriers* Coral Sea *and* Oriskany, *and was actively involved in the modernization of today's carriers. Captain Pierce is retired and lives in Elk Grove, California.*

My father was a Republican in a state with few Republicans and had gotten an appointment to the Naval Academy for my older brother, Ransom. I was only about nine years old when he entered the academy in 1927. He graduated in 1931 with distinction, and because he had done so well our congressman promised an appointment for me at the Naval Academy.

I graduated from the Academy in 1938 and went to the cruiser USS *Chester*, where I served in the gunnery department. I was junior ensign on that ship. I was also trained to become the catapult officer. However, in those days the navy didn't have much money and we didn't steam any more than necessary.

In 1939 I received orders to go to the USS *Buck* DD-420, which was a new destroyer just being built. I went aboard to be an assistant engineer. I also served as commissary officer, assistant to the gunnery officer, the electrical officer, and as a member of several boards, including the examination board for the enlisted men.

While serving on the *Buck* I met my future wife. At the time we were on the East Coast and the *Buck* had orders to report to the West Coast, and I thought one way to stay on the East Coast was to become a naval aviator, and the navy wanted aviators badly at that time. When the *Buck* reached San Diego I received dispatch orders and went to Pensacola. Meanwhile, I got engaged and started flight training in February or March 1941. In July I got married.

I was twenty-four years old. Most of the cadets were much younger— nineteen or twenty. The flying was fun, new, and exciting, and of course we were all wondering what was coming up, because of the wild state of affairs in Europe. I had about two hundred hours of flying by the time I finished my flight training at Pensacola. In October 1941, I was assigned to the type of floatplanes that flew off of cruisers and battleships. They were called SOCs—scout/observation.

In November 1941, I received orders to sail from Los Angeles on 7 December 1941, aboard the SS *President Hoover* for the Philippines. We drove cross-country to Washington state to visit with my brother at Puget Sound Naval Shipyard and arrived there around the end of November. Then we headed down the coast to Berkeley, California, where I had a cousin, Frank Pierce. He had a dinner party on about the third or fourth of December, and at this dinner party I said, "When I come back after the war is over...." And immediately everybody said, "What war?" I said, "We are about to go to war with Japan." It seemed obvious to me at the time that we were about to go to war.

We left Berkeley on 5 December, and on the night of 6 December, we were in Santa Barbara, California, and stayed in a motel. Somewhere along there I received a call from my brother. He said my orders had been changed and that I would not be leaving on 7 December. I was to report in at the naval facility at San Pedro, near Long Beach. So we spent the night at Santa Barbara with the idea of getting up and driving on to San Pedro on Sunday morning to report in.

As soon as we got in the car I turned on the radio, and the first thing I heard was, "...dark smoke clouds rising up over the harbor." I immediately said to my wife, "The Japanese have attacked Pearl Harbor." See, I turned the radio on in the middle of the report, so I didn't hear the words Pearl Harbor, but it hit me that that is what they were talking about.

I reported in at San Pedro, but it was chaos there, so we

Capt. Larry Pierce. During the early days of the fight for Guadalcanal he was the twenty-five-year-old commanding officer of Scouting Squadron Ringbolt, flying very slow SOC floatplanes.

checked into a hotel in Los Angeles. I then sent a telegram to the Bureau of Naval Personnel telling them where I was and asked what I should do. About five days later, I received a telegram back telling me to report to San Diego, to the Transition Training Squadron. I didn't know what that was, but we drove down there and found a hotel. I reported in and was immediately assigned to VP-43, a patrol squadron flying PBYs. They were flying patrols every day, leaving in the morning and coming back after dark. I was assigned to a crew that had a classmate of mine who had already made plane commander. He was the pilot. He had an ensign as his copilot, and I flew as the extra pilot and navigator.

I did that for about a month. Then I received orders to USS *Honolulu*, our newest of the light cruisers. I sailed out of San Francisco with six other ensign pilots for Pearl Harbor. When we arrived at Pearl I was

assigned to a local scouting squadron for temporary duty. I flew antisubmarine patrols in OS2U floatplanes for about a month until *Honolulu*
came in.

When I reported aboard, the senior aviator was Lieutenant Karaberis. He later became an admiral. That was in March 1942. He greeted
me at the gangplank with the most effusive greeting I ever had. I didn't
know it at the time, but I was getting ready to relieve him as senior aviator. I was a lieutenant (jg)—junior grade—by that time.

The commanding officer of *Honolulu* was Captain Hayler, a man I
soon learned to hate. In late May 1942, we were issued winterization
equipment. We got underway and joined some other cruisers and some
destroyers and headed for the Gulf of Alaska. We knew there were Japanese ships heading for that area and we thought they might be heading
for the West Coast of the United States. As it turns out they went into
Kiska, in the Aleutians, about the same time Midway Island was attacked.
We were up there while the Battle of Midway was going on, and on
through the months of June, July, and August, flying patrols. And when
you are flying over water all you have to tell you where you are is your
compass. We had no electronic navigation at that time, so navigation was
very tough.

On *Honolulu* I had eight pilots and four planes. The ship had an
elevator on the stern, and when the planes weren't being used they were
kept in a hangar. One morning we were getting ready to launch and the
weather was getting really bad; visibility was low, and the wind was about
fifteen knots. I said, "Captain, do you want my opinion on the weather?"
He said, "No!" Then he went on to say, "We have instructions not to
use our radios except in emergencies, and being lost is no emergency."
And I thought to myself, "What kind of emergency can be worse than
being lost?"

Of the eight pilots, I had three very experienced ensigns and we all
flew in rotation, and we usually flew two planes together. That day I wasn't
scheduled to fly. The wind had shifted and the visibility had dropped so
that you couldn't see more than a quarter of a mile, and here my men
had orders not to use their radios. Well, of the four planes from *Honolulu* that went out that day two planes came back on schedule, but the
other two didn't. When I thought they were down to about an hour's
worth of gasoline I went to the captain and said, "Captain, they have, at
the most, an hour's worth of gasoline left." At about that time one of the

pilots of the two missing planes come on the radio and asked for a "radio steer." We had a radio direction finder aboard ship, but it was another half-hour before the captain would allow a radio steer to be sent out. About thirty minutes after that we received a message from one of the planes, "Plane out of gas." We heard nothing more. Six months later one of the planes was found floating off the Farallon Islands near San Francisco. It had turned over, but the main float had kept it afloat. We never did find the other plane.

On 7 August 1942, I was launched to spot for the bombardment of Kiska by our ship. All the ships in our task force were going to fire their guns at the island, and each cruiser launched planes to act as spotters. The interesting thing is that we, on *Honolulu*, were told, "We are going to launch you, but we might not have time to recover you. So if you don't get recovered you are to fly to Kodiak." We didn't have enough gasoline to fly to Kodiak, but we were told that there were fifty-gallon drums of gasoline on some of the islands between Kiska and Kodiak. That was pretty vague, and that was the kind of guidance we had.

I sat in my plane on the catapult, and the catapult was trained out away from the ship. I sat there for an hour and the clouds were so low the mast of the ship could not been seen through them. Eventually, they launched us, and as soon as my wingman joined me we circled around under the low cloud ceiling before climbing above it. As soon as we got above the cloud cover we saw a Japanese float-Zero [a Japanese Zero fighter with a float instead of wheels], and I didn't think that was a very good place for us to be, so we went back down below the clouds. By the time we got near Kiska the clouds started breaking up and we went back up to a higher altitude, and we didn't see that Zero again.

Every one of these ships in our task force had classmates of mine as senior aviators on board. One of these classmates and his wingman ran into this float-Zero I just mentioned and got chased by it. My classmate dove back down low and got away from it, but his wingman, who also flew down low, flew up a valley on Kiska and ran into a cable that was stretched across it. He crashed and died.

Anyway, when it came time for our ships to bombard the island it turned into a fiasco. We couldn't see where the shells were landing or which of our ships was firing them. It was chaos! Then the ships retired from the area and I went back to *Honolulu*, landed and was recovered.

We left Alaskan waters in September 1942 and went to Vallejo for degaussing equipment and new radar. And when I went over to Alameda Naval Air Station, I found out we were getting new planes—SOC3s. The SOC3 was a monoplane, but it had engine problems and when fully loaded we couldn't get it off the water. In October 1942, when we were getting ready to leave, we discovered that we couldn't get all four of the SOC3s in the hangar aboard ship. With that we got some old SOCs back and headed down to San Diego, then joined up with a convoy going down to Australia.

On 29 November, we arrived at Espiritu Santo, where I was called over to USS *Minneapolis*. R. Adm. Carlton Wright was the task force commander, and his staff aviator was a Lieutenant Commander Irons. Irons said, "Tomorrow you are going to fly up to Tulagi, land, and I'll meet you up there. Put these parachute flares on your planes, and what you are going to do is take off that night from Tulagi and provide illumination for the task force, because the 'Tokyo Express' is expected off Cape Esperance."

We took off on 30 November—it was a two-hour flight—and flew to Tulagi. There were ten of us altogether from the various cruisers, and we tied up our planes in the harbor and went ashore. I started looking around for Lieutenant Commander Irons, but after about a half hour it became obvious that I wasn't going to find him, so I asked who was in charge. Well, I found out I was the senior aviator present. Lieutenant Pierce, twenty-five years old: just arrived in the theatre and didn't know what was going on. I told my people what Irons had told me we were going to do, so we went back to our planes and got ready to take off. It was night—no lights, no wind, and a calm sea. Only four of the ten planes we had could get off the water. Two hit coral heads. My plane was so underpowered that I couldn't get it off the water, so I sat there and watched this night battle—all these shells flying through the air. The Japanese torpedoed four of our five of our cruisers. We didn't get any of theirs. This was the Battle of Tassafaronga.

I should add that when I received orders to the Asiatic Fleet, I started asking every instructor-pilot I knew, "What do you do in a plane that flies at eighty-five knots, has one .30-caliber gun forward, and one .30-caliber gun in the back with the radioman/gunner?" You know, a plane that flies at only eighty-five knots isn't much of a plane. I asked, "What do I do in a plane like this in a combat situation?" It turns out about all you could do was fly in a slow circle as low to the water as possible. No

**Scouting Squadron Ringbolt lost these three executive officers in one month. From left to right: Bruce Bracket, Leonard Recial, Melvin Hague.**

other plane could turn as tight as a biplane, and that is what the SOCs were—biplanes. And most planes would be flying at a high altitude. At Guadalcanal, I flew almost all of my searches at fifty feet. I lost almost forty percent of my pilots there in one month, and I know at least one of them was flying too high when he got shot down. Two others were lost on night flights. I lost three of my executive officers in one month: Bruce Bracket, Leonard Recial, and Melvin Hague.

In December, I flew over to Guadalcanal and reported to Major General Wood, the senior Marine Corps aviator for Cactus, the code name for Henderson Field. He directed me to fly every day, one flight around Guadalcanal, one flight up to the Russell Islands, and one flight over to Malaita. Malaita was to the east of us. What they were trying to find out was how these Japs were resupplying their troops on Guadalcanal.

Now, what we found during our day searches were these packages— waterproof bags—floating in the water along the coast of Guadalcanal.

SOC floatplane, the type flown off battleships and cruisers to spot for the big guns, among other duties. This type of plane was flown by Capt. Larry Pierce, squadron commander of Scouting Squadron Ringbolt, in the Solomon Islands during the first year of the war.

The Japanese were trying to resupply their troops by dropping these packages in the water from submarines or destroyers, hoping they would wash ashore where their troops could find them. On several occasions I landed and my rear-seat gunner would shoot them up with his gun as I taxied along.

At our base there was a Lt. (jg) George Polk in charge of our refueling station. He asked for some familiarization flights on our SOCs, so we checked him out and he flew okay. Then late one afternoon we received a message that there were two Army Air Force planes north of Savo Island; one was down and one was circling near where the other went down, and we were ordered to send one of our planes up to rescue the downed pilot. It was getting late, so George jumped into one of our planes and flew up there and disappeared. About a week later one of my pilots was flying up near Malaita Island, saw some natives waving at him. He landed near the beach and there was George Polk. George's story was, "I flew up there and saw two planes with lights, so I tried to join up with them, and it turns out they were Japanese. I then flew into a cloud and got lost. Then I saw this island in the dark, tried to land but crashed in the water, and swam ashore." The natives came along and took care of him.

A few days later, I flew over to thank the natives. They took me to their church and sang three verses of "The Star Spangled Banner" in Pidgin English. In the meantime I had written a "man missing in action" report. It was sometime after that that we were informed that George wasn't even an aviator.

George hadn't been back long when he started having nightmares. He started screaming at night. Well, everybody had guns and we were imagining Japs everywhere, so after about three nights of this I asked to have George taken away, and he was shipped home. But maybe George was our hero, because he got home and told all the folks in Washington, D.C., about all these heroic things my people were doing and we got a Presidential Unit Citation as a result.

I know nothing more about George Polk's navy career, but after the war I read in a newspaper that George Polk, then a CBS radio announcer, was found in the harbor in Athens, Greece, with a bullet in his head. Now, CBS has a big award that they give to outstanding journalists; it's called the George Polk Award.*

When I left the Solomons in April 1943, I received credit for eighty combat flights and was awarded the Distinguished Flying Cross. After the war the navy put a message out that if you flew five combat missions you could have an Air Medal, and for twenty-five combat missions you could get a Distinguished Flying Cross. So for my eighty missions I figure I could have had three DFCs and sixteen Air Medals.

I came home in April 1943 and was given thirty days' leave from Alameda Naval Air Station in California. When I came back to Alameda I had orders for commanding officer of a squadron in Alaska flying OS2U floatplanes. I went in to see the chief of staff and told him I didn't want to go to Alaska because there wasn't a war up there. I said, "Captain, I don't mind going back to the war but I don't want to go to Alaska. I want to fly a powerful plane with lots of guns. I was chased by a lot of people when I was down at Guadalcanal; now I want a powerful plane with lots of guns so I can chase somebody."

*Long Island University created the Polk Awards in 1949 in memory of CBS reporter George Polk, who died covering Greece's civil war.*

> "I put in about 2,500 hours in the Corsair, and on my first combat mission I came back with thirty-seven holes in it, so I was a real believer in that airplane."

# Marine Corps Fighter Pilot

## LT. COL. H.A.P. LANGSTAFF, USMC (RET.)

*Lieutenant Colonel Langstaff was born in 1921 in Pittsburgh, Pennsylvania. He graduated from high school in Mt. Lebanon, Pennsylvania, and completed three years at the University of Michigan before being called into the U.S. Navy as part of his reserve obligation (made when he was still in high school). In June 1941, while attending navy boot camp he applied for entry into the naval aviation program and was accepted. After completion of his naval flight training he was commissioned a second lieutenant in the Marine Corps and assigned to VMF-215, flying F4U Corsairs. He completed three combat tours in the Solomon Islands between July 1943 and April 1944, and finished out the war in a training squadron in El Toro, California, before going aboard the escort carrier* Puget Sound, *CVE-113, as part of Marine Air Group Six. Marine Air Group Six included a fighter squadron, a dive bomber squadron, and a torpedo bomber squadron. Mr. Langstaff and his squadron mates flew F6F Hellcat fighters. The war was over by the time they left San Diego in September 1945, to support the occupation of Japan. The* Puget Sound *and its marine air group returned to San Diego in January 1946. Langstaff took a leave of absence to complete his education at the University of Michigan but stayed in the Marine Corps and retired as a lieutenant colonel in 1962. Upon leaving the Marine Corps, he joined Aerojet General Corporation in Sacramento, California, and retired from the company in 1987.*

I did my primary naval air cadet training at the Naval Air Station in Squantum, Massachusetts, outside of Boston. After training at Squantum, we were given a week off to go home. On the train coming back a lady got on in Philadelphia and said, "Isn't it terrible about Pearl Harbor?" That is how I learned we were at war. We had a stopover in New York City that evening, and it was like New Year's Eve in Times Square. The streets were jammed with people reading the news as it flashed around the Times Square News Building.

After Squantum, I was transferred to NAS Atlanta, Georgia, for a month, awaiting transfer to NAS Jacksonville, Florida, which was another big naval aviation training base. After I com-

**H.A.P. Langstaff as a young Marine Corps fighter pilot in the cockpit of this F4U Corsair.**

pleted my training there I requested fighters. I also requested and was accepted as a Marine Corps pilot. My flight instructor at Squantum was a marine captain by the name of Bob Harvey, who later became a brigadier general. His uniform struck me. In those days the officers wore riding boots and a Sam Browne belt. They looked like real fighter pilots. Plus, Capt. Harvey was a great instructor and he took a special interest in me. Another reason I chose the marines over the navy was I heard you had a better chance of getting into fighters if you went into the Marine Corps.

I never had any problems—never had any accidents. I finished my training in Jacksonville in June 1942, and was sent to NAS Opa-Locka, near Miami, for fighter training. We flew the F3F, an old navy biplane—one of the first navy fighters.

I finished my training in Opa-Locka in September 1942, and was sent to NAS San Diego to go through carrier training. No carriers were available at the time, so we were given advanced fighter training in the

F4F Wildcats. After I had completed all my training there, I received orders to go to dive bombers. I went in to see the commanding officer and complained bitterly. He said, "Well then, you'll have to pull somebody else's name out of the hat to replace you." I drew a name out and it happened to be a fellow by the name of Reinhardt "Chief" Leu, who later became a colonel in the Marine Corps. Then Leu went up and complained and he ended up drawing somebody else's name. Leu and I became best friends and flew throughout the rest of the war together.

We did a lot of flying in San Diego in the F4F Wildcat, and after we completed our training there we received orders to go to Santa Barbara. At Santa Barbara we were assigned to a marine fighter squadron, VMF-215. We hadn't even met the group commander yet and the security was tight because a Japanese submarine had recently shelled the coast just north of Santa Barbara. We were issued all of our flight gear, including .45-caliber pistols. Leu, being a great hunter, said, "Come on, let's go shoot some birds down at the beach." So we went down to the beach and started popping away at seagulls. We hadn't fired more than a couple of rounds and we were surrounded by MPs. They hauled us up to the commanding officer and that's how we met him. He took a look at us and just shook his head. His name was Jim Neefus, and he had just returned from the Battle of Midway. Fortunately, he didn't have us court-martialed.

We started our training in the squadron at Santa Barbara, flying F4U Corsairs—one of the first Marine Corps squadrons to receive it. The landing gear on the Corsair had long oleo struts to keep the prop from hitting the ground. The Corsairs had a fourteen-foot-diameter prop and it was found that on a carrier, with those long legs for landing gear, it tended to bounce quite a bit, which made it difficult for the plane to catch the arresting wires. So the navy gave the first production models to the Marine Corps for use in land-based operations.

The early models had a number of mechanical problems such as gas leaks in the wing tanks, and the two-thousand-horsepower engines caused a lot of vibration, which caused the exhaust stacks to crack. With fourteen-foot propellers, there was a great deal of torque created during takeoff. The pilot had to crank in the full right rudder tab and stand on the right rudder pedal to keep the plane straight. Otherwise it would pull you right off the runway to the left. The Corsair was a trail dragger, and the cockpit was fourteen feet back from the nose of the airplane, so you couldn't see ahead until you had enough air speed for the tail to lift off the ground. Being small, I had a terrible time until I resolved the problem with a couple of cushions. Besides the parachute, I sat on a cushion and put one behind me so I could see out of the cockpit and reach the rudder pedals.

My first flight in the Corsair was a thriller. I held on for dear life. But it turned out to be one of the greatest airplanes I have ever flown. I put in about 2,500 hours in the Corsair, and on my first combat mission I came back with thirty-seven holes in it, so I was a real believer in that airplane.

In February 1943, we left Santa Barbara and went down to San Diego and put our planes aboard a cargo vessel. We were taken to Pearl Harbor and dropped off at Ford Island. From there we got our planes ready to fly and flew them over to Ewa, a marine base just outside of Pearl Harbor. We flew out of there for about two months, doing more training.

In Hawaii, the air force and navy squadrons were doing a lot of training. Anybody in the air was open game, and as a result we got in some of our best training. If we were in the air and we saw an air force or navy plane, we usually ended up getting in a practice dogfight. Of course, they were looking for us also. Even if we were on another assignment, if we saw another aircraft—another fighter aircraft especially—we got into a tangle with it, and that gave us a lot of experience that proved valuable later on at Guadalcanal.

In April, all eighteen of the Corsairs in our squadron flew in formation to Midway Islands. We refueled at French Frigate Shoals and managed to get all the planes to Midway. At Midway we did more training and patrolled for enemy shipping and aircraft but didn't find any. We had a couple of planes come in at night and the pilots forgot to lower their landing gear. No one was hurt, but we had to replace the engines and repair the aircraft. Needless to say, our skipper, Jim Neefus, was a little upset.

At Midway we had target craft go out and come back in, simulating the Japanese coming in to attack the island, and we would intercept them. All of this helped us later when we reached Guadalcanal. We were quite fortunate in getting so many realistic training flights before entering combat. I had four hundred hours when I first went into combat, where some of our replacement pilots only had about two hundred hours.

In June 1943, we loaded our planes on another ship and transported them to Espiritu Santo Island. From there, we flew up to Guadalcanal. It was pretty primitive on Guadalcanal, but by that time they did have Quonset huts for us. The food wasn't too good. We made our own showers out of barrels. It was hot and humid, with lots of mosquitoes, and every night a Japanese bomber would come over and attempt to keep us awake. And before he left he would always drop one bomb. Plus, our antiaircraft batteries would try to shoot him down, so we didn't get much sleep.

One night this Japanese bomber—we called him Washing Machine Charlie—hit an old Japanese ammo dump and started that on fire. It lasted for days—shells were flying all over the place and we had to stay in our trenches for two or three days. Some of the shells from this ammo dump went through our Quonset huts.

Guadalcanal had been declared secure by the time we got there, but our ground forces were still fighting up in the hills. We never had any trouble with Japanese trying to infiltrate our camp, but we did later on Munda. We had a small compound nearby with a few Jap POWs—maybe five—and once or twice marines coming back to Henderson Field from fighting in the hills would throw hand grenades in at the POWs. I guess they didn't have any use for Jap prisoners, and of course they didn't take many prisoners to begin with. The base commander put a stop to that sort of thing, and I think they were going to court-martial one of the kids who did it.

We were never attacked by Jap ships or large formations of enemy aircraft while we were on Guadalcanal. We were on the offensive by this time, making attacks further north on islands still held by the Japanese. When we first got there we hadn't taken Munda or Bougainville yet, but we were getting ready to. We were making strikes against Kahili on Bougainville. We flew two types of missions. We would escort the dive-bombers and torpedo bombers when they made strikes. The other type of mission—the ones we fighter pilots really enjoyed—was called a fighter sweep. That is when we would take off without the bombers and fly to our target just above the water so they couldn't pick us up on the way in. Then, just before we got to our target, we would pull up to a higher altitude and dive down on their airfields.

My very first mission was pretty dramatic. I was flying wing on my flight leader, a Maj. Tomes. On the way up to our target his engine quit and he made a water landing near an island. I followed him down and saw him get out of the plane. Once I knew he was okay I climbed back up and rejoined the flight before they got to Bougainville. Maj. Tomes made it to shore and the coast watchers picked him up. He was brought back to Guadalcanal about a week later.

We were always taught to fly with another aircraft, and I was able to pick up another Corsair who happened to be by himself; why, I don't know. He wasn't even from Henderson Field on Guadalcanal, but from a base on another island. We escorted the bombers in and hit our target. We were on our way out and there were Zeros all over the place, making charges into the bombers. All of a sudden the Corsair I was flying with made a one-hundred-eighty-degree turn and headed right back towards the enemy airfield. I didn't know whether to follow him or let him go. I decided to stay with him, and as soon as we left the formation there were Zeros all over us. I got two shots off at Zeros but never hit any of them, and about all I saw after that were tracers coming by my cockpit. Then I smelled smoke and knew I had been hit. We were at about 23,000 feet, so I shoved the stick well forward, creating negative Gs, and dove out of there, pulling out about five hundred feet above the water.

I was able to keep my engine running, but I had another two hours before I would be back at Guadalcanal. I was prepared to make a water landing, and of course all of the other planes were already back at Henderson Field. They thought I had been shot down. However, I did make it back, and as soon as I landed I pushed my rudder pedal over and it jammed because there were several bullet holes in the rudderpost. If I had done that while I was in the air the plane would have been uncontrollable.

After I landed, the first thing I did was get on the phone and find out where this other pilot was located. I figured he was a goner, but he made it back, too. When I got him on the line I called him every name in the book, and he was apologizing all over the place. What had happened, as we were weaving over the bombers to protect them, a Zero had come up under one of the Corsairs from my squadron and shot it down. The pilot was killed and was one of our first losses. The pilot I was flying with got livid and decided he was going to get that Jap, come hell or high water. I couldn't see the Zero, but the other pilot could and he left the formation and headed out after him. Like I said, he made it back too, but he was all shot up just like I was.

I counted thirty-seven bullet holes in my plane when I got back. That is what made me a believer in the Corsair. It could take a beating. That was one of the big things that helped us win the war. Our aircraft were so rugged—with self-sealing fuel tanks and armor plate—they could take a beating and bring you back. You could hit a Zero and it would flame right away.

I was credited with shooting down three Zeros during my three combat tours in the Solomon area. The first one was while we were on a fighter sweep over Kahili on Bougainville. Evidently, they knew we were coming and there were two four-plane formations coming up to meet us. Maj. Tomes and I came up behind two of them and they didn't even know we were there. Tomes got one of them and I got the other. The one I got had smoke coming out of it, then burst into flames almost immediately afterwards. But I didn't stick around to watch it go down because we were taught not to dogfight with Zeros. They were more maneuverable than our Corsairs. So what we did was make a pass and hope we hit it, then kept on going.

The next chance I had to shoot down a plane happened when we were coming back from a mission where we had just attacked Rabaul. I was at about twenty thousand feet with my wingman. I looked down and saw a Zero about two thousand feet below us. He was going back to his base in the opposite direction. From my earlier training he presented a perfect gunnery run where the enemy is below you and going in the opposite direction. You roll over on your back and do what is called a split S, coming down vertically, then settling in behind the enemy plane. I did just that, but when I went to press the trigger, not a single one of my guns would fire. I should have been smart enough to tell my wingman to get the plane, but I was so upset about not being able to shoot him down that I pulled right up beside him. I looked in the cockpit at him and thumbed my nose at that Jap. He was so startled that he did a split S himself and went diving for the water.

On another fighter sweep, again against Rabaul, we were attacked by two Zeros. Now, this was an actual dogfight where we were tangling it up with them. They were trying to get on our tails and we were trying to get on theirs. The one I shot down actually got on my tail and was shooting at me. What I did was back off on my throttle and let him overrun me. He wasn't expecting that, and it allowed me to get on his tail and shoot him down. Here again, I saw smoke, then a burst of flame, as I passed by him.

The third one I shot down was over Kahili on Bougainville. This was kind of a freak situation because he was by himself. It was odd because they usually flew together. I guess he got separated from his formation and was heading back to his field. I was heading back to my field and was getting low on fuel, but I said to myself, "I gotta get another kill." I put full power on and was able to come up behind him. He never even knew I was there. All three of my kills were Zeros. I never had a chance to get one of their bombers.

We went out to the Solomons with about twenty-eight pilots, and I think twelve didn't come back, but a lot of the pilots we lost were due to operational losses. We lost two in one night during a predawn takeoff. With no horizon, you had to go on instruments as soon as you left the ground. One of our pilots took off and spun in immediately off the end of the runway. The second plane taking off—we figure he saw the explosion and was looking down at it as he took off—developed vertigo, and spun in right on top of it. So we lost two planes and two pilots just like that.

We lost two more pilots who tried to destroy an antiaircraft battery. There was one island that had been bypassed, and everybody was warned to stay away from it because there was a Japanese antiaircraft battery that was deadly. On two different occasions two of our pilots tried to put that battery out of action and were lost as a result. In fact, Maj. Tomes, who was my flight leader, was one of them. He was on his way back from a strike and elected to try and knock out that gun and was killed. Then there was our Medal of Honor winner, Bob Hanson—he was killed trying the same thing.

Yes, we lost pilots, but we had replacements coming in. We would be in combat for about three months, then go to Australia for a rest, then come back out for another three months. Each time we came back out for more combat, we picked up replacement pilots. And every time we came back out we had a new squadron commander. Jim Neefus took us out the first time. On our second combat tour we had a squadron commander by the name of Herb Williamson. He was a real gung ho officer. He had to get a kill. He did everything he could to shoot down an enemy plane, but never did. On our third combat tour, Bob Owens took over. He had been the executive officer under Neefus and stayed with the squadron until we returned to the States. He later retired as a major general.

We had a warrant officer, William J. Lane, who was our engineering officer, and the ground crew did such a fantastic job of keeping our planes flying. This warrant officer was an older fellow, in his forties, and being older with all these young kids working for him, he was like a father to them. A lot of them came down with malaria and got sick, but they worked around the clock to keep as many airplanes in commission as they could. And of course, if a plane went down everybody would start stealing parts off it in order to keep the other planes flying. Later, when we were being sent back to the States, a carrier came in with VF-17, a navy squadron, to relieve us. They were put ashore on Bougainville and requested that they be able to use our ground crew for another three or four months. That situation was very controversial because our crew was shot. They needed to get home and have a rest, because they never got R & R like we did. The navy squadron ended up holding our crew for another several months.

I wrote to every one of the parents of the men in our ground crew and explained what was going on, and why they were being held. I told them what a great job their sons had done, and so forth. To this day, when we have a reunion there is one fellow who always pulls out this letter I wrote to his parents. He has carried it around all these years.

All of the men in our ground crew eventually made it back to the States and were reassigned. Of course, some of them got so sick while they were in the Pacific they had to be taken out and hospitalized.

After one of our rest periods in Australia we moved our base up to Munda. We were the first planes to land there after the Seabees completed the field. We had problems with Japanese stragglers sneaking into our camp. They were starving. One day we even found one in our chow line.

From Munda we made attacks against Rabaul. My wingman was George Kross. He was an enlisted man who had come up through the ranks and was an excellent pilot. On one flight we were escorting dive-bombers in on their bombing runs when two Japanese cruisers that were under camouflage came steaming out from the side of the island. I was flight leader and ordered a diving run on them, which was kind of foolish because they had so much more firepower than we did. There were four of us and the cruisers were firing back at us. None of us were hit, but as we pulled up we were jumped by Zeros. My wingman got hit in the wing and his ammo caught fire. There were a lot of rain squalls around and he was able to duck into one of them and put out the fire that way. He joined back up with us and we got the hell out of there. When we got back to Munda he tried to slow his plane down for landing but couldn't get it below one hundred eighty knots. He couldn't control the plane below that speed because of the big hole in his wing where the ammo had exploded.

There was no way he could land that airplane, so he elected to bail out. He got up to about one thousand feet, rolled the plane over on its back and fell out. His chute opened right away, but there was also a good wind blowing. There was a crash boat standing by to pick him up, and before he hit the water he was able to unhook his shoulder straps and one leg strap, but couldn't get the other one off before he hit the water. The wind picked up his parachute and dragged him after it underwater. A fellow from the crash boat dove in with a knife and cut him loose. They pulled him aboard the boat, but he almost drowned. In addition, he had been shot in the arm, but he came around and was okay. The doctors patched him up and he was back flying again.

One day on Munda, one of our marine torpedo bombers came back from an attack. The pilot crawled out of the cockpit and told everybody to disperse because he had a hung bomb and it was armed. The bomb exploded and sent shrapnel all over the place. There was a marine a good distance away when it went off and he was hit in the head. Our flight surgeon had to operate on him right away and remove the piece of shrapnel from his brain or he would have died.

After our third combat tour we came back to the States and most of us were assigned to MCAS El Toro, training new fighter pilots. These pilots had just graduated from Jacksonville and Pensacola. We took them up and trained them further in fighter tactics before they were sent overseas as replacements.

Sometime after that I was assigned to a new marine carrier air group. In other words, this was going to be an all-marine air group, dive bombers, torpedo bombers, and fighters on a navy carrier. However, instead of flying Corsairs, we were now flying F6F Hellcats. We were to go aboard the USS *Puget Sound*, and our air group was Marine Air Group Six. Bob Owens was our air group commander, and had been my squadron commander during one of our combat tours at Guadalcanal.

We went aboard *Puget Sound* but never flew any combat missions. However, we did pull into Tokyo Bay just in time for the surrender ceremonies. We were part of the occupation force, and one of our jobs was to fly over the Japanese airfields and make sure they had removed the propellers from all of their planes. If we saw a plane with a prop on it we were to land and make sure it was removed.

We operated with two other carriers with all-navy air groups, and during air operations all three carriers would turn into the wind at the same time. All during this time that we operated together our marine air group would always be the first to get its planes in the air and recover them. The captain of *Puget Sound*, Capt. Charlie Coe, would always get a "well done" for this, so whenever we pulled into port he made sure the pilots from our air group were the first to go ashore. He always looked out for the pilots because we made him look good.

We went ashore in Yokosuka, Japan, just after the surrender had been signed. I was interested in their aircraft factory there and went to see it. Inside, it was as if they had just blown the whistle for lunch. Everything was just left lying where it was, as if they were going to come back to it. Then I went into some caves nearby in the hills, and in these huge caves they had somewhere around four hundred assembled aircraft engines ready to go into aircraft. What interested me most was the engineering office. There was a large walk-in vault, and inside the Japanese had blueprints for almost every American aircraft we had—complete sets of blueprints. Needless to say, they had spies in our country.

Right after the surrender you wouldn't see many people in the streets. They stayed in their houses, and if you did meet somebody coming down the street, they would never look at you. Of course, they had been taught that we would rape their women. I think they were dumbfounded that we didn't treat them the way they had treated the Chinese, for example.

After we left Japan, we stopped in Hong Kong. While we were there, I ran into a lad who had been in the Royal Hong Kong Volunteer Corps. His name was Bobby Castro and he was Portugese, born in Macao. He was captured by the Japanese when they took Hong Kong and spent the rest of the war as a POW. He told us some real sad tales. He had a married friend in the POW camp and his pregnant wife would come to visit him each day. One day, she tried to kiss him through the fence, and the Japanese took her and put a hose down her throat and filled her up with water until she died. Her husband went berserk after watching that.

When the Japs finally surrendered, the Americans started flying the

POWs out of China. A number of them were in a B-24, and the pilot warned them to stay away from the bomb bay doors. About four of them sat near the doors while it was in the air, and the doors somehow opened. These former prisoners fell to their deaths after having survived all those years in a POW camp.

When we got back to the States I went back to finish my college education in January 1946, but stayed in the Marine Corps and later commanded two jet squadrons, VMF-314, at El Toro Marine Air Base in California, and later a squadron of F4D Sky Rays—a night fighter. I took that squadron over to Japan.

All along, I had planned to leave the service when my children reached high school age. I was stationed in Washington, D.C., and was in charge of all aviation technical training when I resigned. My wife didn't want me to leave the service. She really loved it. And my friend, Gen. Marion Carl, who was a World War II fighter ace and had shot down nineteen Japs, was really upset with me because he thought I would make general if I had stayed in. But it all worked out fine, because all three of my children graduated from college and did well. I went on to work for Aerojet General in Sacramento and retired from there in 1987.

I'm getting off the subject here, but yes, the Marine Corps treated me great. They sent me to Stanford to graduate school where I earned a master's degree, but I never really thought of myself as a military man. I loved the flying, and that was one of the other reasons I left the Marine Corps. It was getting hard for senior officers to get in any flying time. However, I have kept up my support of marine aviation through the Marine Corps Aviation Association, and by going to annual reunions with the remaining officers and enlisted personnel from VMF-215.

---

"I figured my mother didn't raise any foolish children,
so I ducked into the nearest cloud and headed east."

---

# Carrier Air Group Sixteen, USS *Lexington*, CV-16

## LT. CMDR. JAMES ARQUETTE, USN (RET.)

*Lieutenant Commander Arquette was born in Caldwell, Idaho, in 1921. He went to college for two years prior to joining the U.S. Navy in February 1941, at which time he was accepted into the navy's V-5 program. Upon completion of naval flight training and qualification as a carrier pilot, he was assigned to Carrier Air Group Sixteen aboard the USS* Lexington, *CV-16. He later served on the carriers* Bon Homme Richard, Randolph, *and* Boxer. *During World War II his air group was credited with destroying 513 enemy aircraft and sinking 234,850 tons of enemy shipping. Ninety-eight pilots and aircrew were lost during this same time period. Air Group Sixteen was decommissioned on 8 November 1945. Arquette retired from the U.S. Navy in 1963 and now lives in Sacramento, California.*

In grade school I started collecting navy recruiting posters, and even back then I knew I wanted to be a flyer. In college one of my first term papers was about flying for the military. My reason for going to college in the first place was to qualify for the naval aviation program, and Pearl Harbor came along at a fortuitous time for me. I finished my flight training in November 1942, was commissioned an ensign, and was designated a naval aviator. After qualifying as a carrier pilot I received orders to report to a fighter squadron at Quonset Point, Rhode Island: VF-16, which was part of Air Group Sixteen. We flew F6F Hellcats and were assigned to the USS *Lexington,* CV-16.

My first combat mission with VF-16 was against Tarawa in September 1943. That was quite a nerve-shattering experience. I had flown a combat air patrol a day earlier, the last one of the day. We were pretty close to enemy territory, and flying combat air patrol was to intercept any enemy planes that might try to get at our ship.

When I returned to the ship from that CAP, I came in heavy and fast. What I mean is, I hadn't been up long and I had full fuel tanks. It was dusk when I landed and I caught the last arresting wire and my prop went into the emergency barrier. I had to fly that same plane the next morning before sunrise. The prop was fixed and I had to test fly it on the way to the target.

I could see the island in the moonlight. I picked out a target and started firing. At the same time, I could see tracers coming over my shoulder from other planes behind me firing at the same target. That was scary. That, plus few of us had much experience flying at night. That was my first big sortie into combat, and although there were a few pilots in my squadron who had flown off the *Wasp* before it was sunk, most of us were green.

After that we went back to Pearl Harbor. We left again in early October 1943 to make strikes against Wake Island. Then in November we supported the marine landings on Tarawa. That was pretty much the pattern in the early part of the war. We would go out, hit a target, retire to Pearl, rearm and resupply, go out and hit another target, then come back to Pearl. However, as the war moved further out into the Pacific, the navy established fleet anchorages at Majuro in the Marshalls, and later at Ulithi. So instead of going back to Pearl after each strike, we would go to these anchorages to meet cargo and tanker ships, and replenish from them.

Around noon on 4 December 1943, during our attacks on Kwajalein, we were attacked by enemy planes. I was flying wingman for another pilot when my propeller started leaking oil. It covered my windshield and I couldn't see through it. If I had been attacked I would have been in bad shape. When it came time to land I had to open my hatch and lean my head out.

That night we found ourselves surrounded by a bunch of bogies— hostile airplanes. As I recall, there were something like fifty of them. There were no clouds and a bright moon was out. They could probably see us from forty miles out. The ship's company didn't want to open fire and expose our position further, and the enemy planes continued tracking us for several hours without attacking. However, just before midnight, the planes started their attack, and our guns opened up on them; first the 5-inchers, followed by the 40-mms, then the 20-mms. Several torpedoes were launched against *Lexington* by the enemy torpedo planes. We turned to "comb" them—that is, we turned into the oncoming torpedoes and they passed along either side of us. Of course, we were all at general quarters. We—the pilots—were standing by in the ready room, breathing a sigh of relief, thinking we had been missed, when we took a torpedo on the starboard side, aft. The whole ship shuddered like a dog shaking a rat. The ship's rudder was jammed hard over. Fortunately, our smoke tanks on the stern had broken open, so we were creating our own smoke screen and that made us hard to see.

This was at night and we were down at the stern, so we couldn't launch or recover airplanes. Hydraulic rams were set up to control the rudder manually and we made it back to Pearl Harbor that way. Our air group was off-loaded at Ford Island in Pearl Harbor. Then we flew on to Maui and the ship went back to Bremerton, Washington, for repairs. We stayed on Maui until the end of February 1944, when the ship returned to Pearl Harbor and we went back aboard.

In March and April we made strikes against Mille Atoll in the Marshalls, the Palau Islands, and Woleai in the Caroline group. In April, we were sent down to cover landings in Hollandia, Papua New Guinea.

That was the only time I shot down a Japanese aircraft. We had just flown escort for the dive bombers going in to Hollandia. I was leading the second section of our four-plane division. Alex Vraciu, a navy ace, was our division leader. Vraciu was gung ho! He had been with another air group that had been transferred home, but he wanted to kill more Japs, so he transferred to our air group. I couldn't quite understand his gung ho attitude, but some people had it, and I don't knock it.

Anyway, we were to escort the dive bombers, then strafe an airfield. We were supposed to have coordinated strikes, going in with the bombers to divert the antiaircraft fire away from them. We were at about twenty thousand feet and entered a diving turn, changing altitude and direction to make it difficult for the antiaircraft fire to hit us. As we went into the turn, Vraciu steepened his turn. This forced the two other planes with us out of the turn. My wingman found himself in too tight a turn, and had to break off to keep from spinning out of control. As we approached the airfield I realized that Vraciu was still turning, and when I looked down at my altimeter I saw that I was below two thousand feet and coming down at a high rate of speed. I didn't think I could stay with him and pulled out. That was the only time I can remember ever pulling nine Gs in a fighter aircraft, and that is about all one of those aircraft could stand. Normally, you would pull out at three, four, five hundred feet, but not at ground level. By the time I did pull out I was so low to the ground I couldn't turn without clipping a wing on the ground. All I could do was move the nose back and forth and fire at whatever target might be out there.

When I cleared the target I had no idea where the other aircraft in my division were. I pulled up and headed east to our rendezvous point. I had gotten up to about five or six thousand feet and saw three Japanese fighters. They were at my ten o'clock position and a little bit above me. I started climbing towards them, and about then they started turning towards me. I started firing from way out of range, thinking they might be as scared as I was. The Japanese plane that was leading broke off to his right and I followed him. He did a slow roll, and I'll never know why he did that. I kept shooting at him. Smoke came out, and I watched him crash and burn.

I pulled up and saw one of the other planes at my eleven-o'clock position, and below me. I started to dive on him. I had a pretty fair shot at him, I thought, but by the time I was ready to shoot he made a sharp turn to the right and I tried to follow him. Then the next thing I knew, he was behind me. I figured my mother didn't raise any foolish children, so I ducked into the nearest cloud and headed east. That was pretty risky, because that cloud was in a valley with mountains on both sides.

When I did pop out of the clouds, I looked back, and I could see an airplane orbiting the area where I had gone into the clouds. I didn't know where the third airplane had gone, so I figured I had better go home.

In June 1944, we provided air cover for the landings on Saipan. We were part of Task Force 58 west of the island. The small carriers were providing close air support for the marines, and we were out further, providing combat air patrols.

On 19 June we were vectored out to intercept some incoming Japanese planes. This was the beginning of the First Battle of the Philippine Sea—the Marianas Turkey Shoot. My high power blower—the super charger—went out at twenty thousand feet and my engine quit. See, you use a low power blower up to sixteen thousand feet, and then you use the high power blower because the air is thinner up there and you need more air to the engine. We were directed towards the enemy, estimated to be at 25,000 feet, and although my engine started up again and ran well, I didn't want to be a sitting duck at 20,000 feet with them above me, so I turned around and headed for home. I thought I had recognition lights on, but I was a single airplane flying from the target direction at pretty good speed, and heading right for our task force. I felt my plane take a bump. One of our ships was firing at me, so I made a hard right turn and there were more puffs of smoke in my previous line of flight. I then took a ninety-degree change of course, and got out of range. I circled around so that I wasn't coming in from the target direction. When I got back to my ship I found a hole about the size of a silver dollar in one wing root.

We thought we knew where the Jap fleet was, so twelve pilots volunteered to take 500-pound bombs and go out to max range in one search sector. The idea was to hit one or two of their carriers and slow them down enough so the rest of the task force could get in and attack them. Most of the team leaders volunteered. We had about forty-four pilots at that time, and that left the rest of us with few division leaders.

While they were out on this long search, a report came in from a search plane—not one of ours—that they had found the Japanese fleet, 340 miles west, but in a different sector. The report came back that they had a firm position and that it was a carrier task force. Admiral Mitscher decided to launch airplanes, although he realized that by the time we completed our attack and came back it would be dark.

This was a maximum-range effort. We launched at about 4:30 in the afternoon, and were randomly assigned division leaders, since most of our own were already in the air. My temporary division leader was Vraciu, and my wingman was A.H. "Bull" Durham. We had four-plane divisions, and mine was the last one to take off. My wingman had engine problems and had to turn back. After we were airborne we received information that the Japanese carrier task force was one degree of longitude further away, which was an extra sixty miles. That made an extra 120 miles for a round trip. We were all sweating the fuel situation. The bombers,

**Members of Carrier Air Group 16. Pilots Homer Brockmeyer (in the cockpit; K.I.A.), Alexander Vraciu (standing, ace), A.H. "Bull" Durham (sitting, left) and James Arquette.**

particularly, were heavy and had to climb slowly, and they were slow to begin with. Those of us in the fighters had to slow down to stay with them, so we couldn't use our best cruise speed.

We were flying high cover over the bombers, heading west, directly into the sunset. We were scissoring back and forth to make sure no enemy planes were coming from behind us, and the next thing I knew I was all by myself. The bombers and the other fighters had disappeared. They had spotted the Jap fleet and went in for the attack. Vraciu and his wingman had disappeared, and the other division just ahead had disappeared. So I was all alone looking for someone to join up with. Later, Vraciu said that he was jumped by four Zeros that I never saw, and Brockmeyer was shot down.

During that whole battle I didn't see a single enemy plane. Most of them had been shot down the day before, and I didn't think it was smart to be strafing a battleship all by myself.

After the attack we all had to fly home in the dark and it was all dead reckoning navigation over nothing but ocean. I joined up with some other planes and we headed back at about six or seven thousand feet. We stayed fairly high to keep daylight as long as we could. We were flying in and out of thunderheads, navigating as best we could. We were expecting to get back about 8:30 that night. By the time we got to where we thought the task force was, it was nowhere to be seen. There was no horizon and I was experiencing vertigo, as were the other two pilots, so we went our separate ways. I managed to recover from a "graveyard spiral," get straight and level by flying by instruments—what they called needle, ball, and air speed. I then gradually let down so I could see the ocean underneath the clouds.

Thinking I had gone too far, I headed back in the other direction. There was a lot of chatter going on between planes, and a lot of them had already ditched in the ocean after running out of fuel. I was hoping to see some lights or ships. I did manage to hear one little homing direction signal, which confirmed that I had gone too far. I now had a bearing to follow back to the task force.

I found a carrier—not mine—but a carrier. There were so many planes milling around those ships that I was ducking and dodging airplanes the whole time I was there. I entered the landing pattern on one big carrier. I came around and realized there were two other planes trying to land on it at the same time I was. I took a wave-off, and as I came around the second time I saw a big flash along the flight deck. Somebody had crashed and burned on the deck.

After that, I found another carrier—a light carrier—the *Monterey*. I entered the landing pattern and took a voluntary wave-off to let one plane land ahead of me. On the second attempt I finally got aboard and found I had thirteen gallons of gas left, enough for maybe one more pass.

Other planes were making carrier-landing approaches at destroyer truck lights. People were landing in the water beside ships. On the *Enterprise*, the signal officer waved in one plane and two landed. The second one had no lights. One landed short, and the other one landed long, and they both made excellent landings without crashing into each other. Some of the planes in my air group ran out of fuel and landed short into the water. Others ran out of fuel while taxiing up the deck after they landed.

In July 1944, we were relieved by another air group. I guess they figured we needed a rest after that. We had lost quite a few pilots by then. On that cruise, out of forty-some pilots, we lost about half. We were pretty young, and for most of us the war was a big adventure. You expected people to get killed, but not you.

# Navy Fighter Ace

## CMDR. ALEXANDER VRACIU, USN (RET.)

*Commander Alexander Vraciu was born in East Chicago, Indiana, and graduated from DePauw University in 1941. During a summer vacation, Commander Vraciu earned his private pilot's license through the government's CPT (Civilian Pilot Training) program. After graduating from DePauw, he entered the navy and earned his wings as a naval aviator in August 1942. He qualified as a carrier pilot, flying a F4F Wildcat, making eight successive landings aboard the USS Wolverine, a converted excursion ship, on Lake Michigan. He entered combat, flying off carriers in F6F Grumman Hellcats under the tutelage of Lt. Cmdr. Edward H. "Butch" O'Hare, a Medal of Honor winner earlier in the war. Rather than rotate back to the States when the opportunity was offered, Vraciu elected to stay in the Pacific theater of war, serving with three different air groups on six different aircraft carriers, two of which were torpedoed. He survived two ditchings and two parachute jumps during his time in the navy. He made his last parachute jump near Clark Field in the Philippines, after being shot down by antiaircraft fire. He then spent five weeks with Filipino guerrillas before meeting up with the advancing forces of Gen. Douglas MacArthur. He was the U.S. Navy's leading ace for four months in 1944 and concluded the war as the navy's fourth-ranking ace, having shot down nineteen enemy aircraft and destroying twenty-one more on the ground. The F6F Hellcat had a kill-to-loss ratio of nineteen to one during World War II. Commander Vraciu is retired and lives in Danville, California.*

While undergoing naval flight training in Corpus Christi, Texas, Butch O'Hare came and spoke to us after he had won the Congressional

Medal of Honor. Little did I know that I would later be his wingman when he became commanding officer of VF-3, later changed to VF-6.

My first combat assignment was with VF-6 on board the USS *Independence*, CVL-22, a light carrier converted from a cruiser hull. That is when I was picked up by Butch O'Hare to be his wingman, and because he was the squadron skipper, I was able to get in on a lot of the early action. Butch was a natural-born leader who instilled learning and confidence in his pilots. He had a quiet demeanor—never said much—but then, he never had to. We listened to him because of his reputation and experience.

I had my first enemy action at Marcus Island on 31 August 1943. It was relatively tame—just strafing. There was no air-to-air combat but our division did sink a small enemy trawler on the way back to the carrier. We strafed it and it blew up.

Our next action was at Wake Island on 5 October 1943. My radio was inoperative that morning, but I sensed by Butch's actions that something was up. We were on combat air patrol and caught a group of three Zeros coming to land at Wake Island. We were in a perfect position a couple of thousand feet above them. As division leader, Butch had us well trained. He took the far wingman of the three-plane enemy formation, and I took the inboard enemy plane. Butch got his plane on the left but it unexpectedly took him down below the broken cloud layer. I got the Zero on the right—the very first enemy plane I fired on. He was burning good and I practically flew through the pieces.

I pulled up looking for Butch, but kept an eye on the lead Zero that landed on Wake. Butch wasn't around, so I went down and burned the Zero on the ground. While I was shooting up that Zero, I saw a Betty bomber parked, so I pulled on around, came back, and got that one too. After we got back to the carrier I found out that while I was burning the planes on the ground, Butch had run into some other enemy planes, and he got a Betty in air-to-air action.

When we returned to Hawaii, Butch was moved up to air group commander, which caused him to go aboard *Enterprise* with Torpedo Squadron 6 and Bombing Squadron 6. Butch's fighters, Fighting Squadron 6, remained split up on three different CVLs—light carriers. We never saw Butch again after that. Lt. Cmdr. H. W. Harrison became our new commanding officer.

From Hawaii, *Independence* then went south and we hit Rabaul on

**Alex Vraciu, navy fighter ace, climbing out of his F6F Hellcat.**

11 November. A week later, on 18 November, we found ourselves at Tarawa where I got my second enemy plane in air-to-air action—a Betty flying low to the water. Our new skipper, Lieutenant Commander Harrison, led our division, and we were on a CAP when we found a Japanese plane down real low, close to the water. I had the fastest plane that day and I got him.

Then after strafing Tarawa one afternoon our carrier, *Independence*, got torpedoed. We were still underway but streaming oil, so we headed down to Funafuti, seven hundred miles away. We arrived on 23 November, and on the 26th the skipper flew us up to Tarawa. The marines had taken it by then.

We waited there to be assigned to another carrier. A group of us ended up on the USS *Essex* as temporary guests, and it was then that we learned that Butch O'Hare was missing. He was lost forty-five miles west of Tarawa on 26 November 1943. Details were sketchy at first, but what happened was the Japanese were sending in torpedo bombers at night to get at our carriers, and Butch, on *Enterprise* as air group commander, and the torpedo squadron skipper, Lt. Cmdr. Phillips, pioneered what they called "Bat Teams." Two fighter planes were to fly wing on a TBF torpedo plane equipped with radar. At dusk, the carrier would launch the Bat Team and put it in the area where the Betty torpedo bombers were operating. The TBF's radar, theoretically, was to pick up an enemy plane and vector one of the fighters out to intercept it. The concept was primitive and on this particular night things went wrong. The two Hellcat fighters were not launched simultaneously with the TBF and the planned rendezvous never took place. However, the TBF shot down two Bettys and broke up the enemy attack. What happened next has never been fully determined, but the turret gunner on the TBF asserted that a fourth plane—a Betty—got into the formation, and between the Betty and the American torpedo plane shooting at each other, Butch got shot down. I would like to think it was the Betty that shot Butch down, but I don't think we will ever know. Anyway, after Butch got killed, I made a vow to get ten of those Bettys. Pearl Harbor and Butch were my two causes. That might sound corny now, but that's the way I felt.

On 9 December 1943, *Essex* returned to Hawaii and VF-6 was detached. We were then rejoined to Air Group Six on *Intrepid*. At the same time, a call went out to all the carriers for volunteers to practice "Bat Team" intercepts. The officer in charge was Lieutenant Commander Phillips, and during December 1943 and most of January 1944, we trained as a unit. At that time the Japs were way ahead of us in night flying. Then we were sent out on another raid to Kwajalein Island, but by that time the navy had brought out some regular night fighting planes—Corsairs—so we never had to use our night flying training. However, the two torpedo planes we trained with never came back from a raid we later made on Truk Island. Phillips was shot down coming back from the raid, and the other one dropped his bombs on a Jap ammo ship. The ammo ship blew up, and his plane blew up along with it.

At Kwajalein in late January 1944, I was not on the first two flights that day and didn't expect much action. We were flying a combat air patrol over the Roi airfield on Kwajalein, and there didn't seem to be any enemy planes airborne, so we prepared to strafe targets of opportunity—in this instance, parked aircraft on the airfield. My wingman, Tom Hall, and I were towards the tail end of our group of planes as we started going down. Then, out of the corner of my eye, I spotted a string of Bettys flying low over the airfield, so I aborted my dive and quickly got in position to line up on the tail of the enemy formation that was down low on the water, flying over the lagoon. I was taught to wait and get in close before making a shot, but I couldn't wait. That was probably the best deflection shot I ever made, because I barely touched the trigger and the enemy plane caught on fire and crashed into the water.

I then looked up and saw another Betty flying at about three hundred feet. He lowered to about one hundred feet as I came up on his tail. On my first burst, the port engine and wing exploded, and the Betty crashed into the lagoon. Just before it hit I could see people either jumping or being blown out of it and falling into the water.

There were two more up ahead. I let my wingman, Tom Hall, take one of them. The one I went after suddenly headed west, out of the lagoon. In retrospect—I don't know exactly when—I probably caught a round in my hydraulic system, because it affected my ability to fire at the next plane. Only one of my six .50-calibers was firing, and it would only fire a couple of rounds and then stop. I made seven, eight, nine runs at this plane. I lost count after a while. I had to keep charging my guns. Then I must have hit the pilot, because all of a sudden he went into the water. So I got three of them on that one hop. Getting those three Bettys made me feel good—real good!

We had subsequent hops after that, but just to show how ironic things can be in war, my wingman, Tom Hall, was killed the next day on a predawn launch. His Hellcat was spotted forward of mine, so he took off ahead of me. His left wheel appeared to hit a stanchion off the port bow of *Intrepid*, and his belly tank blew up. His plane ended up in a big fireball and fell off to the port side, into the water.

On 16 February 1944, we made our first attack on Truk Island. The two-day operation began at dawn on the sixteenth with a seventy-two-plane fighter sweep. That was a new experience for us—all fighters, with no bombers to protect. We came in low over the water, and then climbed up to about thirteen thousand feet as we neared the atoll. Our main objective was to take control of the air and destroy all enemy aircraft in the area.

Lou Little, my wingman, and I were the last two planes of a twelve-plane group from our carrier assigned to this fighter sweep. There was antiaircraft fire left and right. The leader of our twelve-plane formation started us on our dive to do a strafe. I had learned to always look back over my shoulder before starting down on a dive, and it was a good thing I did this time because there was a group of Zeros coming down on us.

The rest of our planes were too far down in their dive to be of any help, so I turned into the Zeros and broke off the lead plane by shooting directly at him. Below ten thousand feet you don't want to get in a dogfight with Zeros because they will turn and get on your tail pretty darn quick, so you keep your speed up. I managed to keep them well above ten thousand feet. The Zero loses some of its speed and maneuverability higher up, and as he falls off you can come back down on him. I was able to follow three Zeros this way and burn them—blow them up. All of them hit the water inside Truk Lagoon.

While I was at a lower altitude on the last kill, I saw a fourth plane below me, dodging in and out of clouds. Every time I got into position on him, he would go back into a cloud. I played cat and mouse with him for a while, and then I came in out of the sun at him. I don't think he ever knew what hit him. His wing tank and cockpit exploded.

Those four kills raised my personal score to nine, in what I still consider the wildest air-to-air action I ever participated in. Then that night, *Intrepid* was torpedoed in the stern by a low-flying Kate torpedo plane that had followed the wake of our ship. Because of serious rudder trouble *Intrepid* had to withdraw and returned to Hawaii with the aid of a provisional sail.

When we got back to Pearl on the twenty-fourth, Air Group Six was relieved and sent back to the States. I figured I had worked too hard to get out there, and the action was just starting to get good, so I requested to stay. I ran into a friend I had gone to school with, Mark Bright, who was later killed while strafing on Guam, and he introduced me to a Captain Callan. I asked this Captain Callan if I could get a transfer, and he took me in to see some admiral and said, "This guy wants stay out here!" They thought I was crazy. Anyway, they assigned me to Air Group Sixteen—VF-16—on board the USS *Lexington*.

With VF-16 on board *Lexington*, we hit Milli Atoll on 18 March, Palua on the 30th and 31st, Woleai Atoll on 1 April, and Hollandia in New Guinea on 24 April—primarily strafing. At Palau, on three different missions, I destroyed thirteen enemy aircraft on the ground.

Nothing meaningful happened until the end of April, when we went back to Truk. We were escorting dive bombers and were coming in low. That was one of the hazards. Sometimes you had to work down low, protecting the bombers. A group of Zeros tried to attack our bombers, so we went after them and boxed them in—surrounded them so they couldn't protect each other, and I was able to shoot down two of them at their best performance altitude—down low. That gave me a total of eleven. Those Jap planes didn't have any self-sealing tanks, and they just blew up.

I had an afternoon hop that same day that was kind of interesting. Again, we were escorting the bombers. We were at maybe nine thousand feet and just getting ready to start a strafing run. I was cocked over on my left wing and ready to start down when all of a sudden I ran into a barrage of medium-altitude antiaircraft fire. A piece of shrapnel came right through my cockpit. It hit the handle for my landing gear and passed right in front of my face, showering the cockpit with Plexiglas. My hydraulic system was riddled with holes, and my landing gear had dropped down partway. Aborting my strafing run, I was escorted back to the task force by my wingman. My landing gear was just dangling there below the fuselage, and if I had landed it really would have messed up the flight deck, so they gave me a choice; either bail out over the fleet, or ditch alongside a destroyer. I chose to ditch alongside a destroyer. I landed "power-on," using my tailhook to feel the water and land on the back-side of a wave in a heavy sea. Hitting a wave head-on could turn out disastrous. I stepped off the wing into my life raft, barely getting my feet wet, and spent the night on the destroyer *Ingersol.*

I was afraid I would have to stay on that destroyer all the way to Ulithi, and I wanted to get back to *Lexington,* so I asked the captain of the destroyer, Lt. Cmdr. Veazey, if I could send a message to Gus Widhelm on Admiral Mitcher's staff in an effort to get back aboard. That same day, I was transferred from the destroyer back to *Lexington* by high wire.

On 6 June 1944, we left our advance base at Majuro in the Marshall Islands and headed for Saipan. By the eleventh we were off Saipan, and that is where the action started with fighter sweeps around Saipan and Tinian. Our squadron was doing carrier air patrols, followed by escorting our bombers on strikes against Saipan. On the twelfth, I sank a large Jap cargo ship in Tanapag Harbor at Saipan. I came in low and lobbed a 500-pound bomb into the ship right at the water line. It went down pretty fast.

On 14 June, we escorted some bombers to an island north of Saipan, and on the way back at about three thousand feet I spotted a Betty that was at about eighteen thousand feet. I requested permission from the bomber leader to go after it, and he said, "Go get him!" So I dropped my belly tank and raced up to it. I came up underneath her at a sharp angle so she wouldn't see me. Then all of a sudden she dipped her left wing and spotted me. She quickly lowered her nose and started building up speed, but I got her anyway.

On the morning of 19 June 1944, on *Lexington*, our twelve fighter planes from VF-16 were on the flight deck, wings spread, ready for launch. Enemy planes started appearing on our radar, so they launched us to go to 25,000 feet at full power.

On the way up, my wingman, Brockmeyer, kept pointing to my wing. Thinking he had spotted the enemy, I attempted to turn over the lead to him by tapping my head and pointing at him. That's the signal for, "Take the lead, and direct us to the bogies." But he would only shake his head negatively. He did that three times, and I finally had to shake him off in order to concentrate on the task at hand. It was only later that I found out that my wings weren't fully locked. The red safety barrel locks were still extended, which explained Brock's frantic pointing.

A lot of our planes were tired by then—worn out. Paul Buie was our squadron leader. His wingman's engine froze and he had to ditch. He was picked up twelve hours later. Buie was riding behind a brand new engine and pulled ahead until he disappeared over the horizon.

I couldn't go into high blower—twenty thousand feet was my maximum altitude, and I had oil all over my windshield. I radioed back to the fighter director on the ship, and he asked me to bring the group of planes I had with me back to the carrier and circle overhead since the first wave of attacking enemy planes had already been taken care of.

We were at twenty thousand feet and out a bit from the carrier. Then I got a vector from fighter control. From the tone of his voice, it sounded like a good one. The bogies were seventy-five miles away and we headed out in the hope of meeting them halfway.

I spotted three enemy planes a little below us and coming in our direction. In the back of my mind, I figured there had to be more than these three, given the seriousness in the fighter director's voice. Then I saw about fifty or sixty others—a rambling mass of enemy planes about two thousand feet below us—a fighter pilot's dream! They were in a perfect position for me to make a high side run on them. I started on down on the nearest inboard straggler, a Judy dive bomber. Then, peripherally, I saw another Hellcat making a pass at the same plane. I figured we would have collided if I had continued on, so I had to abort my pass. I pulled up and went for another target. And like I said, I had a lot of oil on my windshield, so I had to get in close and I always tried to aim at the wing root and cockpit. Anyway, he burned and went down.

I pulled up, then went back down again and found two more. I got the near one, then dipped a wing, slipped over, and got the second. He went down in a spiral, trailing smoke. The gunner in the back seat kept shooting at me on the way down with his 7.7-mm. I almost felt sorry for the bastard, but just for a second.

Then there was a string of three enemy planes in a row, and by that time they were starting to lower a little bit, but still fairly high, as they approached the outer circle of our fleet. I got to the rear one, and as he nosed over I noticed a black puff appear beside him in the sky. Our 5-inch guns were beginning to open up. Trying to disregard the flak, I overtook him. It seemed I scarcely touched the gun trigger when his engine began to come to pieces. The Judy started smoking, and then began to torch on and off as it disappeared below me.

The next one was one-fifth of the way down on his dive before I caught up with him. This time, a short burst produced astonishing results! Number six blew up with a tremendous explosion right in front of my face. I must have hit his bomb. I yanked the stick up sharply to avoid the scattered pieces. Then I radioed, "Splash number six!"

By then I was getting 5-inch shell bursts all around me from our own ships. I was going to go down after the third one, but he was much further down by that time, and he got hit by our antiaircraft fire. Then all of a sudden, the battle was over. I looked around and all I could see were Hellcats, and pieces of planes falling into the water.

My action lasted eight minutes. I shot down six planes in those eight minutes, and I was told that I only used 360 rounds of ammunition. That meant ten rounds per gun, per enemy plane.

I headed back to the rendezvous area, and all of a sudden some shells were fired by our own ships at us. I said a few choice words over the radio. I would like to think that's what stopped them, but I don't know. Anyway, I landed and flashed six fingers at the bridge as I taxied by. As I remember, VF-16 scored very high in the total number of victories in the "Turkey Shoot," topped only by VF-15 on *Essex*, under the leadership of Cmdr. David McCampbell.

That was the First Battle of the Philippine Sea. The name "Mari-

**Alex Vraciu shortly after the "Marianas Turkey Shoot." He shot down six Japanese planes in ten minutes.**

anas Turkey Shoot" came from one of our pilots, Ziggie Neff. He was telling his story to one of the Intelligence people, and he said it was kind of like a turkey shoot. The skipper of our squadron happened to bring it up again in conversation, and it caught on.

The next day was probably the most hair-raising day of my life. We were in the ready room three times, ready to go. Our submarines had made a couple of attacks on the Jap fleet that was withdrawing westward. Finally, late in the afternoon on the twentieth, one of our search planes located the Jap fleet, and it was decided to launch planes. We called it the "mission beyond darkness." We launched approximately 227 planes, of which fifteen dive bombers, about six torpedo planes (carrying bombs), and about nine fighters were from our air group. I think we lost a good one hundred planes on that mission, counting the ones who ran out of fuel on the way back. We didn't lose that many over the Jap fleet because we had pretty much destroyed their air arm the day before.

Most of our dive bombers had used up much of their fuel by the time they got to the target area. There were nine fighters from VF-16 that went along as fighter cover for the dive bombers and torpedo planes. I had four with me, and four more above us.

It was sort of a botched-up hop. As we got closer and closer to the Jap fleet there was a huge buildup of cumulus clouds, going up to 35,000 feet. The bomber leader started letting down a little bit as he got close to the cumulus buildup, and I lowered too, so as not to get separated by the clouds. The others, topside, maybe should have been watching a little closer, but we were flying in and out of clouds, and they never got into the action. I also lost my number-three man, Arquette. I don't know where he ended up.

All of a sudden, Homer Brockmeyer and I got hit by a bunch of Zeros. We were surrounded by them. From that point on, we were just fighting for our lives. Brockmeyer got hit, and I got the guy who got Brockmeyer. I thought I heard a faint "I'm hit" from Brockmeyer, but I was never able to verify it, but I did see him go down. I also saw one of our dive bombers get hit. The crew bailed out and was picked up the next day.

I was able to get in another good burst at another one of the enemy planes, but couldn't take the time to see if he went down. But I damaged him, I'm sure. As a last-ditch maneuver, I dived on out of the swarm of Zeros. From altitude, we could always dive to get away, because the Zero couldn't handle high-speed diving turns. I headed for the rendezvous area, and I saw a Japanese plane down low, just above the water. God, I wanted to take a shot at him, but I had his friends on my tail, so there was no way!

I had outrun the Zeros that were on my tail and went to the rendezvous area and joined up with one of our torpedo planes that had battle damage. It was close to dusk when I pulled up alongside of him. He was all shot up. He was low to the water, and I wanted him to climb on up to a higher altitude, but he shook his head to say he didn't have enough fuel. He headed towards a group of seven of our planes that were circling low over the water. We had over three hundred miles to go to get back to our carriers. I could hear voices over the radio. One said, "I only have about twenty gallons left. I might as well go in with power on." I heard another say, "I only have thirty gallons left. I might as well land too." I heard later that Task Force 58's search and rescue effort eventually recovered three-quarters of the missing crews.

I pulled up to about eight thousand feet so I could pick up a homing signal from one of our carriers. I still had three hundred miles to go, but I wasn't worried about fuel. All this time, I didn't know what had happened to any of the other guys in my flight. I knew what happened to Brockmeyer, but that was about it. I could hear other crews on the radio. Some were pretty cool; some were breaking down emotionally. It got so bad I just shut my radio off.

I picked up the "A" signal—the homing signal—and saw lights. At first I thought, "Oh my God, I'm heading for Yap!" Then I turned my radio back on and heard the fighter director saying, "Land at nearest base! Land at nearest base!" I wanted to go back to *Lexington*, but it was a melee down there. You have to figure there must have been about a hundred pilots down there who had never made a carrier landing at night. I wasn't worried about myself. I had made lots of carrier landings at night, having been on a Bat Team. Of the seven fighter planes left in my division that night, all seven landed on seven different carriers. I landed on *Enterprise* on my first pass. I taxied forward, and all of a sudden, I felt relaxed. One of the deck crew said, "You better get off the deck right away. They are still landing planes behind you." Then I heard the crash horn! One of the planes landing behind me forgot to put his wheels down and went into the barrier.

One of our dive bombers was shot up, and when he came in for a landing he got a wave-off, which is mandatory, but he landed anyway and killed a bunch of guys, including his wing man's rear seat gunner, who had landed just before him. He caught holy hell from the flight department and some members of the admiral's staff for not taking that wave-off. He will agonize over that for the rest of his life.

We stayed in the area well into July, hitting Guam and softening up the area. Then they said, "Okay, you're going home." Air Group Sixteen was then relieved. We went aboard *Enterprise* at Eniwetok and rode the Big "E" back to Hawaii, followed by a ride on the jeep carrier, *Makin Island*, to San Diego, and thirty days' leave. Because of the six kills I got during the "Turkey Shoot," plus the twelve before that—that made me the navy's leading ace for the next four months.

I came home and the navy had me slated for a War Bond tour, which I didn't want to do. I had gotten married to a girl I had known for only two and a half weeks while I was on leave, and I told her I was going back out, and I did. I was sent to Jacksonville, Florida, for reassignment and got an admiral to call Washington and get orders cut to send me back out to the Pacific.

I got back out to Pearl Harbor, and I was assigned to Air Group Nineteen aboard *Lexington*. That was the air group that relieved Air Group Sixteen when we were sent back to the States after the Marianas operation. I had to hitchhike all over the Pacific to catch up with them at Ulithi. Air Group Nineteen had just been through the Second Battle of the Philippine Sea. They had lost quite a few planes, and *Lexington* had been hit by a kamikaze. That was in November 1944. Nineteen was being sent home and wanted me to go back with them. I said, "God, no! I just spent a month getting out here, and I haven't even flown one hop!"

So Air Group Twenty was brought aboard, and the skipper of the ship assigned me to them. They were doubling the size of the fighter squadrons by that time, so instead of having twenty-something fighters, they now had forty-something fighters per squadron. A lot of that had to do with the escalating kamikaze threat.

On my first hop with VF-20, I burned a few planes on the ground, but not much else happened—no air action. On my second hop that same afternoon, again there was nothing in the air. There was a small airfield near Clark Field on Luzon called Bambam. I went in, dropped my bombs, fired my rockets, and did some strafing down low. I burned one plane on the ground, straightened out a little bit, and went for another. Between the two planes I got hit in my engine oil tank by ground fire. Oil was all over my plane—inside and outside. I quickly opened up my canopy, climbed up to about nine hundred feet, and headed west, not out towards the carriers, but west to get into the hills. It was Mt. Pinatubo where I ended up. I trimmed the plane to fly level, because I knew I had to bail out, but I wanted to get out of the lowlands and get into the foothills, at least. I knew what the Japs did to captured pilots on Saipan—gouging out eyes and cutting off ears before killing them—and I figured I would have a better chance of survival if I could bail out in the hills. I later learned that six other planes off *Lexington* were lost to antiaircraft fire that day.

By the time I jumped I must have been at about five hundred feet or six hundred feet. Before I even had a chance to turn my chute into the wind I landed backwards in a farm field. I made up my mind that I wasn't going to be captured, and had my .45 pistol out. Some Filipino guerrillas came towards me saying, "Filipino, Filipino! No shoot! No shoot!" They got me out of my oil-soaked flight suit and wrapped up my chute real fast. They gave me some clothes and a straw hat and got me out of there because the Japanese had a camp nearby and would be converging on the area within minutes. We went through a village and into some tall grass. A five-year-old boy was our guide. Every once in a while they would pick me up, carry me for a short distance, and then put me down. I asked why they were doing that, and they showed me some bamboo booby traps they didn't want me to step on. They were set so they would rip the calf of your leg off if you tripped one. After I saw one of those, I let them pick me up whenever they wanted.

We got into the hills and reached the guerrilla camp run by Alfred Bruce, a Bataan Death March survivor. There was another American pilot already there. He was a torpedo pilot off *Hornet* who had been shot down about a month before me. His name was Grasscamp, and he was not feeling too good because he had come down with malaria.

A Major Stockton joined us that first day, and I later learned from him that Lt. (jg) D. N. Baker, from VF-20, was killed the same day I was shot down. Major Stockton brought in his dog tags and said his remains had been buried near his plane.

I spent Christmas and New Year's there with the guerrillas at their camp. I occupied part of my time by keeping notes on the air activity over the seven Japanese airfields in the valley below. When the frustration level built high enough I would take pot shots with my .45-caliber pistol at some low-flying Jap planes. I felt better afterwards, but I sure didn't feel good one day when some visiting guerrillas almost matter-of-factly mentioned that the Japanese down below had already killed twenty-two of the men from the village near where I had parachuted, trying to get them to tell where I had been taken.

Then a third pilot was brought in. He was a fighter pilot from another carrier, and we knew from him that General MacArthur's forces had landed on Luzon. The guerrillas put together a force of about 150 men to meet the advancing American forces and provide them with information about what to expect in the area of Clark Field. I asked to go along, and Bruce said, "Sure! Fine! Do it!" The designated leader, Major Stockton, had a recurrence of malaria and I was asked to lead the group. Just like that, I found myself in charge, and I was made a brevet major by Bruce. At the time, I didn't even know what a brevet was. I even had an aide-de-camp I called "Wednesday," to carry my gear.

This group of guerrillas I was with called themselves the USAFFE (United States Armed Forces, Far East). Along the way we picked up thirty more guerrillas. We passed through other camps. Some of them were also hiding American pilots, even some from my ship, but none of them wanted to come with us. They wanted to wait until the American forces reached them.

Where I had been shot down was what the Filipinos call the Southern Tarlac. On our way to meet up with MacArthur's forces we entered an area called the Northern Tarlac. This is the area where the *Huks* [People's Anti-Japanese Army. In Tagalog, *Hukbang Bayan Laban sa hapon—Hukbalahap* or *Huks* for short] had control. We had passed through a number of friendly camps on the way north before entering this small village, Mayuntoc, where I met an American woman living with her Filipino husband. The villagers were making up some rice to feed our men. I was talking to the mayor and this American woman, when somebody brought in some leaflets the Americans had dropped announcing that General MacArthur had returned.

The Japanese were between us and MacArthur's forces. We were reading one of these leaflets that had been dropped when shots rang out below us. Another rival Filipino guerrilla group started attacking our men. One of the men from the rival gang came up to me. His rifle was partly pointed at me, and he asked if I was a *Huk,* because we were coming from the direction of *Huk* territory. I mean it was like the Filipino version of the Hatfields and the McCoys. I put my hand on my .45 and said, "Don't get any ideas! I'm an American. We are not *Huks.* We are on the way to meet the Americans that are coming down this way. I have important information to give to them." He didn't look like he was going to do anything at that point, so I took over and bluffed my way from then on and said, "Okay, take me to your leader." Honestly, I don't lay claim to that phrase. It just came out that way.

On the way, one of our men came running towards me for protection, and they shot him across the middle of his stomach and almost cut him in half. He died right there in front of me. Oh, I used horrible language on those guys! I said, "Here we are trying to get your country back for you, and you bastards don't have anything better to do than kill each other!"

Anyway, the shooting stopped and I was brought together with their leader, a Captain Cleto, who was in charge of this detachment. They put me on a horse, and we rode all night to get to this other camp. The next morning I met with their commander, who was an American—a guy by the name of Hendrickson, who had also escaped from Bataan. This guy was living like Al Capone. He was exploiting all the surrounding villages. If they didn't contribute food, liquor, even women, he would tell them that they would be judged pro–Jap when the Americans came back. Every night I was in their camp these guys would get drunk and pass out. I think they spent more time at the fireside than out fighting Japs.

I put up with that for a couple of days, then said, "Hendrickson, I'm taking my guys and heading on out." However, that night we went on alert. Some retreating Japanese were reputedly going to cross the river just to the west of us, so I was handed a carbine and found myself laying on my stomach, waiting for the Japanese to cross over to our side. As it turned out, they didn't cross over and we didn't have to start shooting, but nobody got much sleep that night.

Late the next morning we started out. We probably had the funniest join-up with the Americans that anybody ever had. Here we went up the National Highway on Luzon, twelve of us on horses, flags waving, bugles blowing, and all the rest—men, women, children, dogs—coming up behind us. Every once in a while an American plane would come down to see what we were doing, and we would wave so they wouldn't shoot at us.

We came up to an American outpost manned by a huge army private. It was obvious that he didn't know what to do with us, so he said, "The sergeant's down the road." So we passed on and soon reached the advanced elements of the U.S. Army's 129th Division, at Paniqui. It didn't take long and a one-star general with an aide in a jeep showed up. His name was General Beightler. All of a sudden, I lost my command and had to say farewell to my aide-de-camp, Wednesday, and the rest of the gang.

At Camiling, I turned over the information I had on central Luzon and made a report about the guerrillas and my experience with Hendrickson. I had to tell my story three times to people in Intelligence.

When I got back to *Lexington* at the anchorage at Ulithi, Air Group Twenty was being relieved to go back home. I wanted to stay out, because I only had two hops before I got shot down, and I wanted to get in on the first Tokyo raids. When we got back to Pearl Harbor I was told that once you've been with the underground—the guerrillas—you couldn't operate over enemy territory again until it had been secured. That's what they told me, so they sent me back home, and I spent the last few months of the war as a test pilot at the Naval Air Test Center at Patuxent River, Maryland.

"The fact that the navy was going to teach me how to fly
and pay me while I was doing it was almost unbelievable."

# Landing Signal Officer, USS *Chenango*, CVE-28

## CMDR. FRANK MALINASKY, USN (RET.)

*Commander Malinasky was born in 1914, in Johnston City, Illinois. Both
of his parents immigrated to the United States from Lithuania in the 1890s.
Upon graduation from Illinois College in Jacksonville, Illinois, in 1938,
Malinasky volunteered for and was accepted into the Naval Aviation Cadet
Training Program. Before the United States entered World War II, he
learned how to fly just about every class of aircraft the navy had in the air
and was flying SB2U dive bombers off the USS* Ranger *until shortly after
the Japanese bombed Pearl Harbor. He served as the landing signal officer
aboard the USS* Chenango *from shortly after the outbreak of the war until
May 1944, and stayed in the navy after World War II until his retirement
in 1963. He now lives in Moraga, California.*

I got out of high school in 1931, which was in the depth of the
Depression. In 1934, I went to Illinois College because I couldn't find a
job. In May 1938, I was about to graduate and I received a flyer about
the Naval Aviation Cadet Program. I didn't even know the navy flew airplanes. The flyer said the navy would take a year to teach us how to fly,
provide us with room and board and uniforms, and give us $50 a month
besides. Once we got our wings we would have to spend three years with
the fleet.

God! I thought that was too good to be true. Hey, in 1938 flying an airplane was a glamorous thing. The fact that the navy was going to teach me how to fly and pay me while I was doing it was almost unbelievable.

I went with my roommate and good friend, Anthony Donat, to East Saint Louis, Missouri—to Jefferson Barracks. We went there in March to take the physical to see if we would be accepted in the program. I only weighed about 118 lbs., and they told me I was too small. I said, "Hell, I didn't know you had to be big to fly an airplane." They couldn't find anything else wrong with me, and the training didn't start until the following July, so the doctor told me to eat a lot and not do much exercise, and just before reporting in he told me to eat lots of bananas and drink lots of milk. So I did what he told me, and then reported to the elimination training program, which was supposed to last about a month. If you could solo by the end of the elimination training program, then you were considered qualified to go on to Pensacola, Florida, for flight training.

I reported to Pensacola at the end of October 1938. At that time Pensacola was the only place the navy had for training pilots. I spent a year there and got my wings in November 1939. After our training we were asked where we would like to go. I said I would like to go into dive-bombers on the East Coast. That was in Norfolk, Virginia, and that's what I got. I started flying SB2Us on the USS *Ranger*. It was the first aircraft carrier built as such, built from the hull on up. Before that carriers had been built from cruiser hulls.

I'll never forget the first carrier landing I made. In those days we had the axial deck. There was a barrier separating the parking area, forward of the landing area, and there were thirteen arresting wires. If you caught the first wire it gave you a long way to stop; that is a gradual stop. But on my first landing I caught the twelfth wire, and that one brings you to a stop in about seventy-five or eighty feet. After that I became pretty good at catching the number two or three wire, and you had to make eight landings to qualify for carriers. But you know we didn't have shoulder harnesses in those days. We only had lap belts and carrier landings were dangerous. If you came in low and slow and stalled, you went into the water and the pilot's head would hit the gun sight and knock him unconscious, and he would drown. When I was on *Ranger* I think we had three fatal accidents like that within a space of three months.

I was in that squadron on *Ranger* until the war started. I remember we were on our way back to Norfolk from Guantánamo Bay, Cuba, where we had been doing gunnery and dive-bombing training. That's when we found out about the Japanese bombing of Pearl Harbor. More significantly, I was engaged to be married on 7 February 1942. It's easy to remember my wedding day, because it was two months after the Japanese bombed Pearl Harbor.

While I was still on *Ranger* the LSO, the landing signal officer, said, "Mal, I think you would make a good landing signal officer." He started teaching me how to wave those flags. This was in Guantanamo Bay just before the war started, and as the Lord would have it, I received orders to become a landing signal officer and got the training in Norfolk, Virginia.

The landing signal officer on an aircraft carrier stood in the left-hand corner (port side), all the way aft, which was the best place for the pilots to see him, and was the officer responsible for giving signals to the aircraft that were approaching the aircraft carrier so that they would be able to come aboard safely. He told them, with flag signals, if they were too high, too low, too fast, too slow, or whether they were lined up properly with the flight deck. He told them if it was safe to cut their throttles and land. If not, he gave them a "wave-off," which meant it was not safe for them to land because their approach was wrong; or there was something wrong on the deck. In that event, the pilot had to put his throttle forward and take his plane around and try again.

The LSO was also responsible for getting pilots prepared for making carrier landings by giving them practice on a simulated carrier deck on an airfield. This way they could make mistakes less likely to be fatal to them and deck personnel. Anyway, those were the duties of a landing signal officer.

Now, if a pilot were to go ahead and land after being given a "wave-off," that was a cardinal sin! It seldom happened. But if it did happen there was always the possibility the pilot would get by with it. There was also the possibility that if the pilot landed instead of taking the wave-off he wouldn't catch one of the arresting wires and crash into the barrier, which was two cables, the bottom one being about three feet off the deck and the top one being about five feet off the deck. The barrier was to protect planes that had already landed and were parked on the forward part of the flight deck. Catching the barrier would bring the plane to an abrupt stop and probably turn it up on its nose.

I remember several instances where planes didn't catch one of the wires and ended up in the barrier even when I gave them a "cut," and I have seen situations where planes have gone over the barrier. When that happened, you really had a conflagration, with planes damaged and people killed.

Once the war got started the navy started radically increasing the number of pilots. But before they went out to a carrier they came out for what was called field carrier landing practice in anticipation of going aboard a carrier to qualify. In other words, the field had a carrier deck laid out on it, and the new pilots practiced landing on that before actually making carrier landings so they would know what they were supposed to do. And there was a LSO there, just like on a carrier. It was while going through training at this practice field that I saw one of the most dramatic accidents of my naval career.

I had just landed and was walking up to the LSO platform where I was going to relieve the fellow who was waving the flags. He was going to take this one last plane aboard before I took over. I think it was an SBD—a dive-bomber. The plane was coming around and got a little bit low, then lower and slower, and then he stalled. He stalled and landed just at the edge of the field and started coming towards the LSO platform. He was veering a little bit to the left, and there were three people there. One was the LSO who was waving the flags, an LSO trainee who was in the early stages of observing, and an enlisted man who was keeping a record of how every pilot was doing. So there were those three and me. I was just coming up towards the platform. The LSO observer ran to the left, and the enlisted man ran to the right. The LSO on the platform just stood there. I guess he thought the plane would continue off to the left, but instead, the plane straightened out and hit the platform. The propeller cut the LSO diagonally in half—sliced right through him. That was the guy I was going to relieve. On a ship there is a net you can dive into in a situation like that, but we didn't have anything like that on a practice field.

After I finished my training I was assigned as LSO on the USS *Chenango*. It had been commissioned on the East Coast and was named after a river. It was one of four light carriers—CVEs—that had been converted from oiler hulls. There was the *Santee, Sangamon, Suwannee,* and the *Chenango*. The *Chenango* had originally been an Esso tanker and proved to be highly desirable as a carrier because it served two functions.

It provided air cover with the planes it had on board, while at the same time having a tremendous oil carrying capacity, so we could refuel destroyers that came up alongside of us. And there was only one LSO on the *Chenango*—me. That was it. If I had broken my leg, I don't know what they would have done. It wasn't till the last six months I was on board that I started training somebody.

LSO

The first experience I had on the *Chenango* was when we took some P-40s—army planes—to the invasion of North Africa. We got off the coast there, just north of Casablanca, and circled around for about twenty-four hours. We were waiting for our soldiers to capture Port Lyautey. After the port had been captured we started launching these army pilots off *Chenango*. The first one crashed in the water. We tried another one, and he crashed into the water. So we decided we had to rethink this thing

**Cmdr. Frank Malinasky, LSO aboard USS *Chenango*, CVE-28.**

and recoach the pilots. We got all the pilots down in the ready room and told them again what exactly the procedure should be. After that, we got all the rest of them off the deck, and we went back to Norfolk. On the way back we ran into some of the worst weather I have ever seen. It damaged the flight deck—actually bent it at the bow.

Cut

**Cmdr. Frank Malinasky, LSO aboard USS *Chenango*, CVE-28.**

When we got back we rested up and got ready to go to the Pacific, which was where all the action was. We passed through the Panama Canal on Christmas Day, 1942. I was sad because I left my wife back in Norfolk. She was pregnant and was going to have a baby in about three months. We went directly to New Caledonia and reported in there for duty. Then we went to Efate and swung around the hook there for a while, and sent our air group to Guadalcanal.

Because my job was landing signal officer, I flew just enough to get my flight time in. You had to fly at least four hours a month if you did administrative work so you could get your flight pay. I never flew and shot a gun in anger during the entire war, but our carrier did participate in the landings at Tarawa, Eniwetok, and Hollandia in Papua New Guinea. I remember the telephone conversation our skipper had with the marine commander of the invasion force on Tarawa. He said, "We've been flying our people all day and they are tired. We would like to give them a rest." The marine commander said, "Captain, my boys are a little bit tired too." Those marines had taken a hell of a beating.

I left the *Chenango* in May 1944. After I left that ship really did see some action. She was at Leyte Gulf and Okinawa. As the LSO on *Chenango* I had a lot of close calls. I had to dive for the net a few times, but I never had to jump in the water. But we did have some planes that landed, then went into the water.

From *Chenango* I went to the Carrier Qualification Training Unit at Naval Air Station Glenview, Illinois. I was the operations officer there until the end of the war. We had two aircraft carriers operating in Lake Michigan, off the navy pier in Chicago. They were the USS *Wolverine* and the USS *Sable.* I was responsible for getting the pilots assembled and sent out to the ships in the numbers called for. We would give them eight carrier landings on the *Sable* or the *Wolverine*, then send them directly off to the squadrons.

I was just brand new married when the war started. I wanted to be home, but I enjoyed being aboard ship, and I enjoyed flying. But I don't feel like I missed out on anything by being an LSO. That was an exciting job and I had a lot of responsibility. The only person who had more was the commanding officer of the ship. In some ways I feel like I missed out on something by not having flown combat during the war, but then if I had I might not be here now to tell my story.

# Sailor/Marine/Fighter Pilot

## CAPT. BERNARD W. PETERSON, USMCR (RET.)

*Captain Peterson was born in Long Beach, California, and enlisted in the
U.S. Navy in February 1941. After boot camp he received training as an
aviation machinist's mate and was assigned to Torpedo Squadron Three
(VT-3) aboard the USS* Saratoga. *The* Saratoga *was torpedoed by a Japanese submarine in January 1942, and VT-3 was transferred to the USS*
Yorktown *after it had taken a bomb hit at the Battle of the Coral Sea and
returned to Pearl Harbor for repairs. VT-3, aboard* Yorktown, *suffered
the loss of all of their torpedo planes and most of their crews during the
Battle of Midway in June 1942. VT-3 was then rebuilt with new crews
and the new Grumman Avenger torpedo bombers, and boarded the USS*
Enterprise *in time to join the opening days of battle for Guadalcanal. In
January 1943, Aviation Machinist Mate Second Class Peterson received
orders to flight school. During the first half of 1944, he trained in SBD-5
dive-bombers, and he trained in F4U Corsairs during the second half. He
returned to the Pacific as a U.S. Marine Corps fighter pilot, flying F4U
Corsairs with VMF-223. Captain Peterson returned to civilian life after
World War II, but volunteered to return to active duty during the Korean
War, again flying F4U Corsairs.* (This oral history was taped by William
J. Shinneman, 27 July, 1991, and is part of The Oral History Archive,
American Airpower Heritage Museum, Midland, Texas.)

My father, who was a World War I veteran, died in 1940 and the
family broke up. I had a year to go in high school, but before my mother
and brother moved to Montana to live with her sister I had her sign a

letter for me so I could join the navy. However, the navy asked me to finish high school before enlisting. So that is what I did: I finished high school in January 1941 and swore into the navy in February.

When my training as an aviation machinist mate ended in August 1941, I was assigned to Torpedo Squadron Three (VT-3) on board the USS *Saratoga*, which at the time was home-ported at San Diego—North Island. In October we headed out to the Pacific for what was supposed to be a resupply of Hawaii's outer islands—aircraft parts, personnel, heavy equipment, and whatever.

We went to Midway, and we may have gone to Wake; I can't remember. The other carriers, *Enterprise* and *Lexington*, were doing the same thing. Then, in December 1941, *Saratoga* left to go to Bremerton, Washington, for

Bernard W. Peterson when he was a young sailor early in the war.

its annual thirty-day overhaul. The air group was taken back to North Island, San Diego, while the ship went on up to Bremerton. However, *Saratoga's* stay at Bremerton was cut short and it came back to San Diego on 7 December 1941, to pick us up. They were alerted that an emergency was pending. We heard about the bombing of Pearl Harbor while at the hangar on North Island while getting ready to go back aboard *Saratoga*.

We loaded aboard *Saratoga* all night long, and at ten in the morning on 8 December, we pulled out for Pearl Harbor. We arrived at Pearl five days later, dropped off some supplies, and took on some others. Then we took on a marine fighter squadron and headed for Wake Island. We were going to be the support group that would save Wake Island from the Japanese. We had an oiler with us that was capable of doing only about twelve knots, and for that reason they slowed the whole task force to the speed of the oiler, which made us late getting to Wake, and the Japanese took it before we got there. We were then diverted, along with the marine squadron we had on board, to Midway. We dropped off the fighters, which were used against the Japanese in the Battle of Midway at a later date. Most of them were lost during that battle.

We came back to Pearl and then were assigned to patrol duty the first two weeks of January 1942, about five hundred miles southwest of Pearl Harbor. One night, while doing about seven knots to conserve fuel, we took a Japanese submarine torpedo. We were in a roll to starboard and the torpedo came in under the port side blister. *Saratoga* bounced like a toy boat when that torpedo went off.

It was the darkest night I have ever seen. I was in my bunk, which was forward and below the hangar deck. I dressed and ran down the hangar deck to a boat pocket on the port side. That was the quickest access I had to get to my plane, which was tied aft on the flight deck. The torpedo had hit right underneath the ladder I took to the flight deck, and part of the deck was missing. When I stepped to go up the ladder I went into thin air until I grabbed a piece of chain and pulled myself back up. Some other guys laid some planks across the opening and I made my way up to the flight deck. By that time we were listing twenty-seven degrees, and we all thought the ship was going to roll over.

Again, there was no light whatsoever. It was black and the entire deck and all the planes were covered with crude oil as a result of the torpedo hit, so we were slipping and sliding. I had to hold on to an arresting cable to pull myself up to the planes on center deck. The planes were creaking, and the lines holding them to the deck were about to snap. It seemed like we were in that position for the longest time until the engineers flooded some starboard compartments and brought us up to not quite an upright position. Then what seemed like tons of waste rags were brought up to clean the crud off the deck, the planes, and us.

The destroyers and cruisers in our task force opened up on the Japanese submarine, dropping ash cans—depth charges—and it surfaced. Our ship had floodlights on it and we were firing at it point-blank. It surfaced just four hundred or five hundred yards off our port position and everybody swore we got her, because we could see bubbles, debris, and oil come up. But as history shows, it wasn't even harmed. It got away but was sunk later in the war.

Anyway, we crippled on back to Pearl Harbor and went into dry dock, and our air group was off-loaded at Ford Island in Pearl Harbor. A patch was put on the hole so we could get her on back to Bremerton. There was so much damage that they figured she would be there for three or four months. The hole in the side of the ship was big enough to drive a train through.

In May 1942, *Lexington* was sunk at the Battle of Coral Sea, and *Yorktown* had taken a hit from a 500-pound bomb and was on its way back to Pearl. Admiral Nimitz was preparing the fleet to meet the Japanese invasion fleet heading for Midway Island and we were all alerted. The *Yorktown* went into dry dock and yard workers were working around the clock to repair the damage. We—Air Group Three—were loading our gear on board the *Yorktown* while it was still in dry dock. We were replacing Torpedo Squadron Five, but they left the bulk of their enlisted support crew on *Yorktown*, while the bulk of our enlisted support crew was left ashore to service Torpedo Squadron Five. There were just a few key enlisted personnel from VT-3—experienced mechanics, radio repairmen, and so forth—who came aboard *Yorktown* with the rest of the squadron. It was a real mix-up.

We sailed out of Pearl on 29 May. *Enterprise* and *Hornet* had a day-and-a-half lead on us. We caught up with them several hundred miles north of Midway Island.

On June 4, at 0830, our squadrons took off. We had twelve TBDs— torpedo bombers. The squadron commander was Commander Lance Massey. He was leading our twelve planes with their twelve pilots and their twelve rear seat men. I was not flying that day. Had I been flying that day, I would have been flying with an enlisted pilot, Harry Corl. But Lloyd Childers was flying with Corl that day.

The torpedo planes went out about noon and were at a fairly low altitude. They were jumped by swarm after swarm of Jap Zeros. The first one to be shot down was our skipper, Lance Massey, who was seen getting out of the cockpit and on to the wing root of his plane. His plane was on fire and crashed. One after another of our TBDs were shot down. All of the torpedo squadrons suffered considerable losses. All those guys knew they were on a suicide mission. The sole survivor from the torpedo squadron on the *Hornet* was an Ensign Gay. From our squadron, the two surviving pilots were Wilhelm Esders and Harry Corl. They both got shot up and ditched. Lloyd Childers, the rear seat gunner, got into a raft with

Harry Corl. Childers was wounded but Corl wasn't. Robert Blazier was Esders' rear seat gunner, and he was hit pretty bad. He spoke only a few words to Esders before he died in the raft. Out of twenty-four men in our squadron who took off, twenty-one died.

The torpedo bombers diverted the Jap Zeros from the slow-climbing SBDs, allowing them to get into position to carry out their attacks on the four Jap carriers, subsequently sinking all four of them. Very few Jap fighters intercepted them because they were so preoccupied with the low-flying torpedo planes.

Over the years I have been in touch with Wil Esders. He went a full thirty years in the navy and came out a commander. He started out as an enlisted man—got his wings as a second class petty officer.

The *Yorktown* was hit by bombs and torpedoes. I helped with the casualties and fought fires on board until Captain Buckmaster ordered abandon ship. Most of the crew went over the side on the starboard side—the high side. We were afraid the ship might roll over, the list was so bad. I was picked up by the destroyer *Benham*, then transferred to the cruiser *Portland* the next morning. On June 7, I was again transferred, this time to the submarine tender USS *Fulton,* and got back to Hawaii on 8 June.

With some new planes and some new pilots and crews, we went on board *Enterprise* on 15 July 1942, and set sail for the Tonga Islands. There we met the marines who were assembling for the invasion of Guadalcanal, which was scheduled for 7 August 1942. The landings went off very well, but the Japs came in during the night and sank four of our cruisers, and the supply ships had to leave prematurely. We had to go south several hundred miles to Espiritu Santo to get away from Japanese aircraft.

About 23 August our task force headed back up, and on the 24th we were about two hundred miles east of Guadalcanal, near Stewart Island. *Wasp* had retired south to refuel. *Enterprise* and *Saratoga* were the only two American carriers in the next battle, the Battle of Stewart Island. *Saratoga* was not hit during the battle, but *Enterprise* sustained three hits. My friend Harry Corl, whom I mentioned as one of the survivors at Midway, got shot down. He didn't make a water landing; it was a high-speed, high-angle crash. Harry and one of the crewmen died. The gunner, Delmar Wiley, survived. He went down with the plane and had a hell of a time getting out. When he did get out and came to the surface there was the plane's life raft sitting there, but he was wounded. He had taken some 20-mm shell fragments in the legs. I guess he floated around for the best part of a week before he came ashore on a little island east of Bougainville—the island of Carteret. The natives found him and he spent a total of seven months on that island before he was rescued.

I was knocked around on the hangar deck when *Enterprise* was hit. A Chief Mortz had told us all to get away from the center of the hangar deck because if we took a bomb that went off below the hangar deck it would bulge and we would all be flopped up to the overhead and be left pasted up there. So by his recommendation we all went to the outboard side on the hangar deck, and we did take a bomb hit. It came in and blew up below the hangar deck in the chiefs' quarters, and like Chief Mortz predicted, it humped the hangar deck. We, being on the outside of the hangar deck, didn't shoot up as high as some of the others who hadn't heeded Chief Mortz's warning. They hit the overhead and were killed. Their bodies cushioned our fall when we came down. I sustained flash burns, shrapnel wounds, and a concussion. We all treated our own wounds. I pulled some shrapnel out of my leg with some long-nosed pliers and poured sulfa powder in the wounds.

I climbed up a ladder to the flight deck and made my way through men lying there with arms and legs missing. A couple of them were pulling themselves over to the side of the ship to commit suicide. I guess they couldn't bear the thought of living in that condition.

I went over to a 20-mm gun crew that knew me as a qualified gunner and they strapped me into a 20-mm, and for the remaining two or three minutes of the attack I was shooting at diving Val dive-bombers. The original gunner had sustained an eye injury from a direct hit he had made on a bomb being carried by a Jap plane. The bomb and the plane had exploded just above the superstructure of the ship and debris had rained down on everybody.

We had a lot of fires; we had a lot of casualties and holes in the flight deck. We patched the holes up with steel plates so we could take on planes coming back from their flights. Some of our planes came back and made night landings on the damaged deck, and others were diverted to *Saratoga*. The next afternoon we buried seventy-four sailors at sea, wrapped in clean mattress covers, weighted down with 5-inch shells.

The next morning all the planes that had landed the night before were dispatched, some directly to Henderson Field on Guadalcanal, but most of them were sent to Efate. This included our six TBFs that had made it back. Our skipper, Commander Jett, was the first to take off in our squadron for Efate, and because he was going to be operating on a remote field we had loaded up his plane with spare parts, tools, personal gear of the three crew members, and even some depth charges in the bomb bay. He had a pretty heavy load when he took off. When he got airborne he just dropped over the bow. Then we saw him come up and make a clearing turn. His wing tip hit the water and he cartwheeled in. The second plane did the same damn thing, and so did the third. They were just off our port side by a few hundred yards as we cruised by. The depth charges shook loose and started going off. There were nine men in the water when this happened and many of them were killed. Of those who survived, many had lifelong internal injuries. The fourth plane took off with no problems and landed in Efate.

We left the area on 25 August for Tongatabu. The navy had a repair party down there. On the way I was put on the salvage crew—the acetylene cutting crew—cutting out all of the bomb damage. I was also put on the party that went down to the starboard aft quarter, below the metal shop where the ship had taken a bomb hit. We had a hole in the ship at the water line, and we were taking water. We shored it up with timber and mattresses, and we had the pumps running twenty-four hours a day, trying to keep the water out of there. The first thing we did when we got to Tongatabu was to flood the port ballasts to raise the starboard side and pull all the debris out. The upshot of all that was we got a temporary patch put on and headed back to Pearl.

When we got back to Pearl on 15 September 1942, they put us in dry dock. *Saratoga* had taken another fish [torpedo] at the end of August, right after *Enterprise* had left the area, and came crippling in right behind us. So *Enterprise* and *Saratoga* were in dry dock together. *Enterprise* left dry dock and pulled out without us on 16 October 1942, for the Battle of Santa Cruz Island, which took place on 26 October. That is where *Hornet* got sunk and *Enterprise* took three 500-pound bomb hits. It retired to Noumea, New Caledonia. At that time it is accurate to say we had no operational carriers in the South Pacific.

When *Saratoga* got out of dry dock our squadron, VT-3, came aboard and we left for Noumea in the middle of November 1942. By December 1942, *Enterprise* and *Saratoga* were the only operational carriers in the Pacific, but by that time most of the major battles for the

Solomons were over and we didn't have much to do. December was laid-back.

A year and a half before, I had requested naval flight school. I wanted to be a pilot and I was selected and received my orders. I boarded *Lurline*, which during peacetime had been a luxury liner. Most of the passengers were wounded marines from the fighting on Guadalcanal. A lot of them were walking wounded. I would say the bulk of them were Section Eight candidates—psychos. My heart really went out to those kids, some of whom had what the marines called the "thousand-yard stare." There was no way to describe what they had been through. They played poker on deck and the money they played with was gold teeth they had knocked out of Japanese with their rifle butts.

The end of January 1943, we arrived in San Francisco. I had to resign from my enlisted rating and became part of the navy's V-5 naval reserve program. I was making between $175 and $200 a month with my flight pay as an enlisted man. While in flight school, I had to go to $75 a month cadet pay.

I graduated from flight school on 21 December 1943, and about six of us from my class went into the Marine Corps as second lieutenants. The rest went into the navy as ensigns. After graduation I was sent to Florida for dive-bomber training. I had led myself to believe I was going to be a Corsair fighter jockey and never even considered that the Marine Corps would assign me to anything but Corsairs. When I finished on 1 April 1944, I had flown the SBD-5 Dauntless dive-bomber 118 hours. Then on 7 June 1944, my big day arrived. My orders were to report to VMF-524, a marine fighter squadron with Corsairs.

By Christmas 1944, I was on the high seas with about two thousand ground crunchers from Camp Pendleton and three dozen marine pilots on the USS *O.H. Ernst*, a marine transport. We let the ground crunchers off at Russell Island, then went on up to Guadalcanal where all the pilots went into a pilot replacement pool. I was there for a week or two and went all over the island, visiting all the battlefields to familiarize myself with what I had not seen back in August 1942. Then I, along with five other pilots, was assigned to VMF-223, which was supposed to be up on Bougainville. I checked in but the squadron had already flown their Corsairs off to Samar in the Philippines via Finschhaven, Biak, and Peleliu.

A DC-3 came in and we all loaded on board and flew on up the

**Bernard W. Peterson as a U.S. Marine Corps fighter pilot, flying F4U Corsairs later in the war.**

same route our squadron had taken. We were about a week behind them. On Peleliu we were in a BOQ [bachelor officers' quarters] tent area. One night a group of Japanese came down from Babeldaop in boats and made a suicide attack, landing about one hundred yards from our tents. They came through with bayonets and grenades, blowing up tents and jabbing at the beds whether there was anybody in them or not. They got to our planes and started blowing them up with grenades. I slept through the whole thing. The next morning a young marine came in and shook me. He said, "Wake up sir, wake up! Are you all right?" He thought I was dead. I asked him what was wrong, and he told me about the suicide attack, and that we had a bunch of our men killed. All sixty-seven of the Japs were killed, and I slept through the whole thing.

We flew on to Samar where we joined VMF-223. We were supporting the army on their landings at Cebu Island, Panay, Mindoro, Mindanao, and Negros. We were flying two and three missions a day in our Corsairs, loaded with napalm, 500-pound bombs, 1,000-pound bombs, and rockets. Most of the information being given to us on our targets was coming from guerrillas. We attacked a lot of airfields the Japanese had on Mindanao. We got a lot of planes on the ground, but some of them were dummies meant to suck us in so they could shoot us down with their antiaircraft guns.

During the landings on Cebu, I was able to get a Sally bomber on the ground just as she was taxiing to take off. We made repeated runs over Cebu, and I was just pulling out after dropping my last load when I came out under one of our B-25s just as he caught it right in his engines.

He flew apart right in front of me, and I flew through some of the debris. Nobody got out. I flew back to Samar, another three hundred miles, with that vision in my mind. That stuck with me for a long time—the vision of that B-25 crashing. That was in March 1945.

Sometimes we would catch the Japs out in the open. The army would push them into a ravine or up against a cliff and they wouldn't give up, so we would fly in and lay napalm on them and just kill thousands of them that way. You could see them burning and squirming down there on the ground, but they wouldn't give up, and it was easier for us to go in and hit them with napalm than let the army go in and take losses. It was horrible; we would go in day after day and lay loads of this stuff on them.

In June 1945, four squadrons of us—there were about twenty to twenty-five planes per squadron—flew up to Clark Field on the island of Luzon. We refueled there, stayed overnight, and the next morning flew with a marine navigation plane 1,200 miles, all the way up to Okinawa. We flew through a hell of a thunderstorm and got spread all over the map. A.H. Perry, who was very close to me, never came out of it. There was a telegram for him when we got to Okinawa, saying his wife had just given birth to a baby girl.

There were two Jap airfields that we had taken over on Okinawa. There was Yontan and Kadena. We couldn't find Yontan. It was raining, the marines were still fighting the Japs at the south end of the island, and it was getting dark; and here we had about one hundred Corsairs trying to land. We finally found Yontan, and the airfield was about seven thousand feet long, but the first half went uphill, and the last half went down.

We were landing two planes at a time so we could get everybody down quickly. When we got to the end of 3,500 feet of runway we were braking because we didn't know there was another 3,500 feet of runway. The tower never said a thing.

From Okinawa, we were fighting the kamikazes between Okinawa and the island of Kyushu in southern Japan. We went on raids clear up to a field called Miyazaki on the east coast of Kyushu. Col. Howard King was the commanding officer of our squadron, VMF 223. We also had Ken Walsh, an enlisted marine pilot, the first marine ace of the war from Guadalcanal.

In July we hit Miyazaki. We came in from fifteen thousand to twenty thousand feet. We were using the first proximity-fused bombs. A flight of four planes that went out the day before with these new fuses got wiped out when one of the bombs went off prematurely. They had been improperly armed. The ground crews worked all night on the arming problem, and the next morning we were the next flight out and were hoping they had fixed the arming problem, which fortunately they had.

I was the wingman for Colonel King. We came in through cloud cover in the early morning and we caught hundreds of Jap planes on the ground. With these new proximity-fused bombs, we just wiped them out. I then strafed the control tower, and on the way out I still had eight 5-inch rockets on my wings, so I fired them at a destroyer or destroyer-escort-sized ship that was firing at us just off the coast. I laid all eight rockets broadside into her. She either went down or was at least hurt badly.

At Buckner Bay on Okinawa, we had all the ships assembling for the invasion of Kyushu, planned for the following November. We already had a field marked out for us on Kyushu that VMF-223 was going to work out of once the island was taken.

However, the war ended and we lost about six people from our squadron during the celebrations. They were driving down the runway in a jeep when it flipped over into a rice paddy. They broke their necks and drowned in six inches of water. A couple of them were aces and had been out there for a couple of years.

The celebrations killed a lot of other people on Okinawa. All the ships were firing off their ammunition, and it was raining down on our Quonset huts. In mid–September, I left Okinawa, and by November I had my orders to inactive duty, which they did with all the reserve pilots who had gone through the training program. The war was over for me.

> "Burial at sea is a very solemn, sad occasion when you see friends tipped over the side and into the water."

# Aboard the USS *Bailey,* DD-492

## STANLEY M. HOGSHEAD

*Stanley Hogshead was born in 1919 in Hudson, Iowa. He entered the U.S. Naval Academy in 1939 and graduated three years later in 1942 with the first of the three-year war classes. After graduation he was immediately assigned to a new destroyer, the USS* Bailey, *DD-492. The* Bailey *was commissioned in May 1942 and received nine battle stars as well as the Navy Unit Commendation before being inactivated in December 1945. Mr. Hogshead left the navy in 1947 and spent the rest of his working life in the banking business, ending up as the president of an independent bank. He is now retired and lives in Roseville, California.*

The USS *Bailey* was a new Bristol Class destroyer. While on her shakedown cruise she struck a ledge outside Casco Bay, Maine, damaging her starboard propeller and its shaft. When I caught up with her she was in dry dock in Boston Navy Yard where she was having the damage repaired. After we got out of dry dock we patrolled all up and down the East Coast of the United States for a few months on antisubmarine patrols. Ultimately, we went through the Panama Canal and up to San Diego, then San Francisco, where we drew foul weather gear.

After we drew the foul weather gear we went first to Kodiak Island, then west to the Aleutian Islands, with our first stop being Dutch Harbor. Dutch Harbor was mainly a supply base for ships and airplanes that were operating in that area. But the weather was such that there wasn't much air reconnaissance taking place. There were constant storms, constant fog, rain, hail, snow, and mountainous seas that made it difficult even to get out of the harbor.

In early March 1943, we formed a task force with *Salt Lake City*, which was an old heavy cruiser, *Richmond*, which was an old light cruiser, and three other destroyers—*Coghlan*, *Dale*, and *Monaghan*. *Bailey* was the flagship of our destroyer screen, and we had as our screen commander Commodore Ralph Riggs.

We left Dutch Harbor around the middle of March 1943, and proceeded west. The reason we left was because the U.S. had broken the Japanese naval code and we knew that the Japanese were going to attempt to reinforce and resupply their troops on either Attu or Kiska, possibly even attack Dutch Harbor, and we were sent out to prevent that from happening.

We were in a scouting line with all six ships about fourteen thousand yards apart on a straight line, heading in the same direction, and each ship looking for any vessel that might appear on the horizon. As I recall, the USS *Dale*, which was an older destroyer, was on one end of this scouting line. While we were at general quarters on March 26, she reported a ship, maybe two ships, hull down, meaning way over on the horizon. R. Adm. Charles McMorris was in charge of our task group. I don't remember what formation he ordered us into but it was a battle formation of some sort, and we were already at general quarters, which was customary when in enemy waters. Every station was manned, and every watertight compartment was dogged down, meaning the doors were closed and locked.

This alert came at about 0600 and my battle station was in "Plot." Plot is roughly amidships, centerline, just one deck below the water line, and just forward of the forward fire room. The forward engine room is just aft of the forward fire room. Also forward of us on the same deck was the crew's mess hall. Forward and above that were the frozen food locker and the ship's commissary, just to give you some idea of where I was.

The size of Plot was about fifteen feet by fifteen feet and on each bulkhead were banks of electrical equipment. In the center of the room was the main battery computer. It was called the Mk. 1 [Make 1] Mod. 2 [Model 2], one of the earliest fire control computers. It was huge by today's standards, standing about waist high and measuring thirty inches square. The computer controlled the elevation and train of our main battery, which were four 5-inch .38-caliber single-mount guns.

When the only door to this room is closed and "dogged down" it becomes a watertight compartment. During general quarters the door is of course closed and the room is sealed off from the rest of the ship. During general quarters you don't leave your watch station under any conditions. It is a court-martial offense if you do. As I recall, there were about seven or eight other men in that room, besides myself. After we had been there for about thirty or forty minutes it came over the sound-powered telephone system that instead of one or two Japanese vessels, there were several, and shortly thereafter it was determined that we were faced with two heavy cruisers, two light cruisers, and four destroyers. I don't remember the class of the Japanese destroyers, but they were modern destroyers and the cruisers were also modern. There were also a number of transports, which turned away when the action started.

As the range between our two forces closed the Japanese, with their 8-inch guns, began to fire at approximately twenty-four thousand yards; that's twelve nautical miles. We were going at about thirty knots, and *Bailey* didn't start firing until she was about fourteen thousand yards from the enemy; that's seven nautical miles. That's a long, looping projectile trajectory for a 5-inch gun. But as the range closes, the trajectory of an 8-inch shell becomes pretty flat. It wasn't too long before we would cease fire for a moment or two, and when we did we could hear the 8-inch shells landing in the water close to us. The skipper was following standard evasive procedure, and this went on and on. Those of us in Plot would look at each other and wonder how long it would be before we got hit. I recall some of the men commenting, "How can they miss us?" Well, it wasn't too long before they did hit us. We heard a loud, terrible explosion pretty close to us. We found out later that that was a near miss that opened up a seam between the forward fire room and the plotting room, where I was. Remember, the forward fire room was the compartment immediately aft of ours. Water started to come into our compartment; not a big, heavy stream but enough to make us take off our life jackets to try and plug the leak and stop the water from coming in.

It was now after 1000 and we had been at battle stations since around 0600. That is a long daylight engagement, and it turned out to be even longer. In fact, it was the longest daylight engagement our navy had ever fought. Then we received word over our sound-powered phones that *Salt Lake City* had been hit and was losing speed. Finally, we received a message from *Salt Lake City*: "My speed zero."

I'm not sure if Admiral McMorris ordered us to make a torpedo attack, or if Commodore Ralph Riggs asked permission to make a torpedo attack. Either way, three of our destroyers split off from *Salt Lake City* to make the torpedo attack, while the fourth remained behind to guard *Salt Lake City*. We went to maximum speed and headed directly for the Japanese heavy cruisers. We got to within a range of 9,500 yards, and for the 8-inch guns on those cruisers it was hard for them not to miss us and they didn't. They were pounding us pretty good with near misses until they got a direct hit, getting us in our crew's mess hall and the frozen food locker, killing or severely injuring almost all our forward damage control party who had been stationed there. It was a deafening explosion, and at about that time we lost power. Our lights went out and water was coming into our compartment. There we were, standing in the dark with only two battle lanterns that gave off an eerie, bluish light, which allowed us to see instrument dials and the outlines of people but nothing beyond that. We couldn't even see our own hands.

We ended up taking four hits from 8-inch shells, two of which did not explode. The trajectory was so flat that when some of the shells hit the deck they ricocheted off.

As our speed slowed until we were momentarily stopped, the captain ordered our torpedoes fired at a range of 9,500 yards. This is an extreme range for a torpedo attack to be successful. I don't think we got a hit with any of those torpedoes, and from what I have read the Japanese didn't acknowledge any hits. But the threat of the torpedoes caused the Japanese admiral to break off the action.

We got some power back and were able to make ten knots or twelve knots—something like that. That was the end of the action, but there we were, still in the plotting room with the water coming up above our ankles, and boy was it cold. The water temperature was 33 degrees. We knew we were badly damaged but we didn't know how badly. At approximately 1230, when the action had ended, we were given permission to open the door to our "tomb" and escaped to the main deck after having been locked in there for well over five hours.

My memories are of standing there wondering if I would live another second or make it out alive, and holding hands and praying with several other guys. That's pretty hard to forget. But as we left our compartment we realized that for the moment we were safe. However, I was astounded to see that both our forward fire room and forward engine room had been flooded, and that we had only six inches of freeboard between the water and our main deck.

There was one little sailor by the name of Raymond. I don't remember his first name. He had red hair and was a regulation sailor if there ever was one. He was always clean and his hat was always on square. He always did his job and took great pride in whatever he did. You could always count on that fellow. His steaming station was in the forward engine room, but during general quarters his station was in one of the gun turrets. After the battle was over he went to the forward engine room, and when he looked down all he saw was water. I will never forget what he said when he saw that, "Oh my God! My cleaning station!" In other words, he didn't care about the ship's safety; it was his cleaning station that he was most concerned about.

We then headed back to Dutch Harbor where a destroyer tender made some temporary repairs. We

Ens. Stanley Hogshead, graduate of the U.S. Naval Academy, Class of '42. He was on USS *Bailey*, DD-492, at the Battle of the Komandorski Islands.

had a number of war dead on board as a result of the action we had been through off the Komandorski Islands, so from Dutch Harbor we went to Kodiak, where there was a cemetery. Our dead were transferred there for burial.

The captain of *Bailey* at that time was John C. Atkeson. He was a wonderful man. He was dearly loved and respected by every man on that ship. He performed wonderfully with that ship and for his actions at the Battle of the Komandorski Islands, and bringing his ship out he won the Navy Cross.

After that, we went back to Mare Island for four months, where we were literally rebuilt. While we were there and undergoing repairs, Capt. Atkeson was relieved and we received a new skipper by the name of Lt. Cmdr. Malcolm Munger.

After completing our repairs, we had sea trials and then another six weeks for the training of our many new crew members. Then we were ordered to Pearl Harbor and thence to New Zealand. *Bailey* then was a part of the close fire support group for the landings on Tarawa, Saipan, Tinian, Eniwetok, and finally Peleliu, where we had been assigned as close fire support and later to antisubmarine patrol.

It was while on antisubmarine patrol one moonlit night that we received word that Japanese planes were approaching, and it wasn't long after that that we were attacked. *Bailey* was attacked by a single Japanese fighter plane. Since we were silhouetted by the moon, he could see us by coming in from the opposite direction, but we couldn't see him. I could hear him cock and test fire his guns—*tat-tat-tat-tat*, and right after that his attack began. I was in the main battery directory; I had the best seat in the house.

The fighter came in from either the starboard or the port beam, depending on our heading, and a couple of times he made runs from stem to stern. He struck in the 40-mm gun nest, which was just aft of midships. My gunnery officer back there reported that he had been hit and was going off-line, meaning he had to hang up his phone and get somebody to take his place.

We were firing at the enemy fighter but not hitting him because he was zooming in and zooming out. He was coming in so fast he was past us before we could get a gun on him. After he left the area, we began to count our losses, and they were extensive. You wouldn't believe the number of machine gun holes we had in that little destroyer, including in the main battery director, just a few feet from where I was standing. My 20-mm antiaircraft officer was killed six feet from me. He had been to my wedding, and I had to step over his body to get out of my battle station.

I don't remember how many killed and wounded we had, but on a destroyer you only have three hundred and some odd number of men, and you get to know each other pretty well. We headed back to Pearl Harbor for temporary repairs, but what to do with the dead? We had a doctor on board who took care of the wounded, many of whom were later transferred to a cruiser. Our skipper finally requested permission to bury the dead at sea, and permission was granted. I had always played the trumpet, and I kept it with me on board ship. The skipper asked me to play taps for the burial at sea. Burial at sea is a very solemn, sad occasion when you see friends tipped over the side and into the water. After that was over, I went to my room, fell into my bunk and wept.

That was the last action I was in. When we got back to Pearl Harbor we had some temporary repairs made. Machine gun bullets had hit some of our torpedoes and depth charges, none of which exploded. Why they didn't, I'll never know. We then went back to Mare Island for three months of repairs and I was transferred to new construction, the USS *Newman K. Perry*. We were in Guantánamo Bay, Cuba, when the war ended. We then went back to Charleston Navy Yard and I got transferred, this time as flag lieutenant to Admiral Frank Beatty, Commander Destroyers Atlantic Fleet, based in Portland, Maine.

I was with the admiral for about a year. I then decided that navy life was not right for my wife and family. I had a daughter and another baby on the way, and neither my wife nor I wanted to live the navy life any longer. I resigned from the service in 1947.

# USS *Arizona* Survivor

## JOSEPH K. LANGDELL

*Mr. Joseph K. Langdell was born in 1914 in Wilton, New Hampshire.
After his graduation from Boston University in 1938 he went on to become
an officer in the U.S. Naval Reserve. His first assignment as a young ensign
was aboard the USS* Arizona, *BB-39. He was on temporary duty ashore
at Ford Island when the Japanese attacked Pearl Harbor on 7 December
1941, and can list himself among the few survivors as a result. In July 1942,
Langdell left for "new construction" aboard the USS* Frazier, *DD-607.
While aboard the* Frazier, *he fought in the Solomons and the Aleutians.
He ended the war as a lieutenant commander attached to Commander Fleet
Service Force, Seventh Fleet, in the Philippines. He now lives in Yuba City,
California.*

I went into the navy in late 1940. I read in a newspaper that the navy
was looking for officers for the United States Naval Reserve. I went on
a cruise on the battleship USS *New York* for thirty days, and then went
on to the midshipman school at Northwestern University. I got there in
January 1941, and was commissioned an ensign in the United States Naval
Reserves in March 1941.

Because I came from the cold country of New Hampshire, I always
wanted to go to a warmer area and to be a naval officer on a battleship.
So I told the navy I wanted duty on one of the battleships stationed at
Pearl Harbor and was assigned to the USS *Arizona*, BB-39. I reported
aboard *Arizona* on 26 May 1941, and was assigned to Second Division,
which was number-2 turret, and that is the one that took the bomb hit

that blew her up when the Japanese attacked Pearl Harbor on 7 December 1941.

In August 1941, I was given temporary duty with the Fleet Camera Party. The Fleet Camera Party was the detail that took motion pictures of the ships as they fired their guns at targets. We went to sea in an old four-stack destroyer that towed a sled, which carried the target. When the ships fired their guns at it there would be a splash in the water, and the film would show if the splashes were short, long, or to the left or right. The reason they needed an ensign on the Fleet Camera Party was because that was the lowest rank in the navy that could work a slide rule. There were no computers in those days.

There were about fifty or sixty ensigns on *Arizona,* and if I hadn't been picked to go on temporary duty and had been at my battle station on *Arizona* when the Japanese attacked Pearl Harbor, I would have been down in the powder room of the number-2 turret where the 1,800-pound armor-piercing bomb exploded and blew up the forward part of *Arizona.* My not being aboard is what saved my life.

The complement of *Arizona* was somewhere around 1,500 sailors, marines, and officers. One thousand one hundred seventy-seven were killed that day. There were approximately 335 survivors, and out of those 335 there were about sixty who were ashore, either on temporary duty like I was, or on liberty, at service schools, or carrying out normal ship's routine.

When 7 December came I was asleep at the Bachelor Officers' Quarters on Ford Island, which was right next to Battleship Row, and about three hundred yards from *Arizona.* The building was shaking and I didn't know what was going on. I asked my roommate if the army was having a practice with their planes that morning. The building kept shaking and we knew something was wrong, so we got up, put some clothes on, and went down to the water's edge, about one hundred yards from *Arizona,* and watched the ship blow up in seven seconds and sink in nine minutes.

We were absolutely helpless. There wasn't a thing we could do. *Arizona* was gone. I then went with some others to the head of Ford Island, where we saw some survivors beginning to come ashore. We helped them out of the water and they were all black from oil. On some, the skin was peeling off from being burned. We then took them to the Naval Hospital there on Ford Island. At the hospital there were two lines. A doctor at the head of the first line would decide if a man could be quickly returned to duty or be sent to the second line for further treatment.

A few days later, after the metal on the ship had cooled from the fires, I was having breakfast when an officer from the command ship, USS *Argonne*, came in and asked if there were any officers from *Arizona*. I raised my hand and this officer said, "After breakfast, you will go down to the dock. There will be a motor whaleboat there, twenty men, and some sheets and pillowcases. Go over to *Arizona* and remove all of the dead bodies that are topside, above the water line." So that is what we did. It was a gruesome task. We had to use ropes to get the bodies down from the bridge. After we got all the bodies wrapped in sheets and into the motor whaleboats, they were taken ashore for identification and burial. We took all the arms, legs, heads, and other body parts and put them in pillowcases, and they were also taken ashore. Then we took brooms and dustpans and swept up all the smaller pieces.

When the armor-piercing bomb went through four decks and 5.62 inches of armor and exploded in the powder room of the number-2 turret, where I would have been had I been on board ship, it ignited over five hundred tons of ordnance which was stored there and in nearby powder rooms. That explosion destroyed *Arizona* in seven seconds, causing the bridge to fall into the cavity created by the bomb, and the ship to sink within nine minutes.

Several days later, divers were sent down to explore the inside of *Arizona* and to take out bodies. However, it was found that the

Ens. Joseph Langdell, one of the few survivors of USS *Arizona*, after it was sunk at Pearl Harbor.

ship was so wrecked and there were so many pieces of sharp metal that it proved impossible. In fact, one diver lost his life in the process.

On 4 December 1976, a group of twenty-one ex–crew members of the USS *Arizona* formed the USS *Arizona* Reunion Association in Tucson, Arizona. Over the past twenty-four years I have held every office except member of the board of directors. Presently, I am the treasurer. During this twenty-four-year period, we have grown from twenty-one people to over five hundred. This includes survivors of the battleship *Arizona*, relatives of crew members, and anybody who was ever a crew member since it was commissioned in 1916. In the last few years we have included a category called Friends of *Arizona*. They are people who are interested in our ship.

In 1981, I wanted to organize a private memorial service for the association at the USS *Arizona* Memorial at Pearl Harbor—a ceremony just for us, so we could pay tribute to the men who were killed that day. I worked that out with the National Park Service, and now every five years since then we have gone to Pearl Harbor for our private memorial service. We also have a private memorial service at Punch Bowl Cemetery in Honolulu for all the men from *Arizona* who were killed that day and are buried at Punch Bowl.

I just came back from this year's reunion in Tucson, Arizona. There were about sixty people there. Six were survivors of the ship when the Japanese attacked Pearl Harbor, and the rest were crew members who had served aboard before Pearl Harbor, plus relatives and friends of *Arizona*.

There are sixteen survivors of *Arizona* who wanted to go and join their shipmates when they died, and so they have. Their ashes have been interred inside the hull of the ship. When my time comes I will do the same.

# HMAS *Canberra* and the Battle of Savo Island

## LT. CMDR. MACKENZIE JESSE GREGORY, ROYAL AUSTRALIAN NAVY (RET.)

*Lt. Cmdr. Mackenzie Gregory was born in Geelong, in the state of Victoria, Australia, in 1922. In January 1936, at the age of thirteen, he joined the Royal Australian Naval College at Flinders Naval Depot in Victoria as a cadet midshipman, entering a four-year training program. Because of the imminent threat of war, instead of graduating at the end of 1939, this group of cadets was sent off to join the fleet in August of that year. The war started for Mac (as he likes to be called) when he was seventeen, in September 1939, when he joined the crew of the cruiser HMAS Australia. Aboard* Australia, *he served in the Atlantic, Mediterranean, and Indian Oceans before returning to Australia. He arrived in Melbourne on 7 December 1941, just as the United States was about to enter the fray as a result of the Japanese attack on Pearl Harbor. Mac stayed in the Royal Australian Navy until 1954, serving as aide-de-camp to His Excellency Sir William McKell, Governor General of Australia from 1950 to 1953. After leaving the navy he worked for many years in marketing before going back to university and getting a bachelor's degree in health administration. He worked in that field for fifteen years. Mac is now retired and lives in Melbourne, Australia.*

I joined HMAS *Canberra* in December 1941, which then escorted the last Australian troops into Singapore in February 1942. They were soon to become POWs of the Japanese, to suffer over a long time, and many would die. We were lucky to pass through Banka Strait, call at Batavia [modern-day Jakarta], and escape the ever-tightening Japanese noose.

American naval forces were now appearing in Australian ports and in the Pacific. With General MacArthur's escape from the Philippines to Darwin, Australia, he arrived in triumph in Melbourne to become commander of Allied forces in the area. He was seen by many as the potential saviour of our country. The press of the time played up this role and almost gave the general a divine presence, or at least god-like qualities. It suited the Australian Labor government of that time, and the then prime minister, John Curtin, forged a working partnership with MacArthur. As a country, we could not defend ourselves, and I have seen copies of Japanese plans to invade Australia.

It was necessary to have a strong partner, and a huge American troop buildup resulted, with Australia becoming the major base to act as a springboard for U.S. and Australian forces to take up MacArthur's Island-hopping strategy. However, not everyone considered MacArthur all sweet-

Lt. Cmdr. McKenzie Gregory, Royal Australian Navy, and survivor of the sinking of HMAS *Canberra*, one of four Allied cruisers sunk at the Battle of Savo Island in a matter of minutes.

ness and light. Many of our service people thought him very arrogant, a person who loved the limelight, and who did not give credit to Australian troops for what they achieved. Our servicemen's success scarcely rated a mention in MacArthur's press releases. It was Australian troops in New Guinea who were the first to stop the Japanese onward rush, but no one would have known it at the time.

U.S. troops in Australia were much better paid than ours. Their uniforms were of better quality and much smarter than Aussie ones; and their ways with women were more sophisticated. Their manners were better than those of locals, and the Australian girls, to a large degree, reveled in this wonderful attention they received from U.S. servicemen—flowers, chocolates, nylon stockings—a new heaven had arrived on our shores.

At the time, it was common to hear about the Yanks in Australia, "They are overpaid, oversexed, and over here." American servicemen were sometimes heard to remark to their Australian counterparts, "Look, Aussie, we are taking your girls away from you." The Aussie response was, "Don't worry, Yank, you are just sorting them out for us." As a result, there were some ugly clashes between American troops and Australian army veterans who had just returned from the Middle East theatres. In both Perth and Brisbane, fights between the two groups erupted and some deaths occurred.

In 1942 or 1943 an American serviceman in Melbourne murdered a number of local women, and until he was caught, tried, and eventually hung, there was a tremendous outcry amongst the local population in Melbourne.

While I was serving aboard both HMAS *Canberra* and HMAS *Shropshire*, we carried some U.S. naval officers who ran the cipher machines. The Americans did not trust us to run them. These American officers reckoned it was the best duty in the Pacific, as we had liquor in our officers' mess, unlike U.S. ships. One of these American officers, Ens. J.W. Vance, was killed aboard *Canberra* at the Battle of Savo Island.

Both of the Australian ships I served on in World War II worked as part of U.S. Naval Task Forces, and as a bridge "watchkeeper," I needed to change from a Royal Navy system and ways of maneuvering in a fleet formation to the U.S. Navy system. The first few times I had to change to a new course while part of a U.S. Navy task force were an absolute nightmare. It meant literally picking up the fleet formation steaming on a specific course, rotating that force through fifty degrees,

**HMAS *Canberra*, one of four Allied cruisers lost at the Battle of Savo Island in August 1942, a time when the Allies were losing ships faster than they could be replaced.**

and then putting it down again so that the ship maintained its relative station just as if you had not moved. You had but a few seconds to calculate where you had to move to, what course and speed you needed to use, then, on the command "execute," take up the new position, being careful to avoid any collision as all the ships milled around to take up their new spots. It put a few years on me very quickly, but I soon became adept at taking up a new position within the task force.

I always found members of the USN to be very generous, although as an Australian unit, when it came time to restock our food, etc., we naturally tended to be last in the queue when supplied by U.S. forces. The fast pace of the Pacific war often meant that the Australian supply ships would be very far behind our needs, so of necessity, we had to rely on our American friends.

HMAS *Canberra* was a unit in the force being used to cover the landings at Tulagi and Guadalcanal in August 1942. On the night of August 8–9, we were part of the southern screening force there to prevent any Japanese surface forces reaching our transports unloading at Guadalcanal. HMAS *Australia* led HMAS *Canberra* and USS *Chicago*, with U.S. destroyers *Patterson* and *Blue* as our antisubmarine screen. The USS *Ralph Talbot* and USS *Blue* were stationed outside Savo Island as seaward radar and antisubmarine pickets to alert the Allied naval force to any approaching Japanese ships. The fact that they failed in this duty to sight and then report enemy forces set the scene for the subsequent debacle.

The northern screening force was made up of U.S. cruisers *Quincy*, *Vancennes*, and *Astoria*, along with two destroyers, USS *Helm* and USS *Wilson*. I was the officer of the watch—midnight to 0400—and we were steaming a course of 130/310 degrees at a speed of twelve knots, altering course 180 degrees to starboard without signal, on the hour. The night was dark. Savo Island was cloaked by rain, and aircraft could be heard overhead.

At 0143 we were on the 310-degree leg. I was very conscious of the time and had to call our navigating officer at 0145 so that he could fix our position and oversee the change of course at 0200. *Patterson*, our port-screening destroyer, reported by TBS (talk between ships), "Warning, Warning! Warning! Strange ships entering harbor." As *Canberra* was not fitted with TBS, we did not hear this warning. *Patterson* also tried to warn us by signalling, using a small blinker tube.

We were suddenly under torpedo attack, altering course and increasing speed to dodge the onrushing Japanese torpedoes. We went to action stations [general quarters], and the captain quickly arrived on the bridge to assume command. Ahead, star shells illuminated the scene, and soon aircraft flares fell to our starboard. The navigating officer took over from me, and as I was leaving the bridge for my action station in forward control, just above the bridge, we came under severe gunfire from several Japanese cruisers on our portside, only a few thousand yards away.

A hail of shells struck the ship. A shell exploded on our portside just below the bridge and decapitated the gunnery officer, Lieutenant Commander Hole. The captain was mortally wounded, and several other bridge officers and enlisted men were badly wounded, including two midshipmen, Bruce Loxton and Neil Sanderson. The torpedo officer yelled, "I've been shot in the bum!" I had escaped to forward control and, using my binoculars, could make out Japanese cruisers firing at us. They were very close, and I exclaimed, "My God! This is bloody awful!"

There was another explosion amidships. The 4-inch gun deck was hit, and our Walrus aircraft was ablaze on its catapult. The plotting office, near the bridge, received a direct hit and Midshipman Johnstone was sent off to investigate. He returned quite shaken, reporting, "Schoolie is all over the wall." The "schoolmaster," in charge of the plotting room, had been blown to pieces.

I had remained unscathed. Another enemy hit landed just aft of my position. Able Seaman Oliver, standing beside me, moaned suddenly and fell to the deck. He had picked up a shell fragment in his head from the explosion. I gave him a shot of morphine but he was a very sick young man. I lost track of him after that and never saw him again.

The ship had lost power and was slowing down. We were taking a noticeable list to starboard. For *Canberra*, the war was over. Only about three minutes had elapsed since we assumed action stations.

Forward control was abandoned, and I went off to help dump ammunition from the blazing 4-inch gun deck and assist in moving the wounded. I went below decks to the sick bay to seek out any wounded down there. There were no lights and I only had a torch [flashlight]. It was dark and eerie, and incoming shells had created havoc. I found a sailor with his arm blown off. His arm, with a ring on one of the fingers, was lying on the deck, but he was in shock and didn't realize it was his arm until he saw the ring. Then he collapsed and I administered morphine.

The ship suddenly shuddered and we assumed a greater list. I felt sick in my stomach. I feared we were about to capsize and I would be trapped. Then the ship steadied and the wounded man was taken up on deck. It was raining heavily, but it felt wonderful to be on the deck in the open again, and away from the confined space several decks below the waterline.

I had purchased a gold-wired, embroidered officer's cap badge in England from the famous naval outfitters Gieves whilst undertaking my sub lieutenant's course. The local badges were stamped out of metal and quite inferior to my special cap badge. When I rushed to my action station I had tossed my cap in a corner and donned my tin hat. I now decided to retrieve it. However, when I scrambled up to forward control, [there was] no cap, no badge—only a large hole where I had left it.

On my way down, I came across two sailors carrying a body on a stretcher. They lifted off the patient to drain away the accumulated blood. I now recognized Midshipman Bruce Loxton. He had a ghastly wound, and I wrote off his chances of surviving on the spot. He was conscious and said, "I will be all right." He did recover and went on in the RAN to retire as a commodore, and to author the book *The Shame of Savo*.

I still had my binoculars around my neck and used them to make out USS *Chicago* exchanging fire with *Patterson* before correct identification was made. Captain Bode of USS *Chicago*, after taking criticism about his actions at Savo, took his own life, and the Battle of Savo Island claimed yet another victim.

**A copy of Japanese occupation money the Japanese planned to use in Australia once that country had been conquered.**

At one point I tried to go aft to reach my cabin, where I kept a few treasures packed in a small panic bag, but it was not to be. I could not pass through the fierce fires burning amidships. Then *Patterson* secured aft to remove crew members from that area, and *Blue* came along the portside forward, and I eventually jumped across to her deck and was taken to the transport *Fuller*. Like everyone else, I lost everything, having only what I stood in, a pair of overalls, underwear, socks and boots, plus my binoculars. Those I still treasure. My clothes were all soaked, but we were all quickly issued with Marine Corps shirts, trousers, and boots. I guess I at least looked like a U.S. Marine for a short time, a proud member of the U.S. services.

On board *Fuller*, lying on the deck, was a Japanese airman who had been shot down, then fished out of the water. He was badly burned and a shoulder had been shot away. He was sedated, but I think he died the next day.

We had burials at sea. *Canberra* had lost eighty-four crew members, including our captain. Another 110 were wounded. Before the action started, we had 819 officers and sailors aboard *Canberra*. The Northern Cruise Force had *Quincy*, *Astoria*, and *Vincennes*, all sunk, with a loss of close to one thousand officers and sailors—an absolute debacle for us.

For the Japanese it was a stunning victory, but they had not completed the job; they didn't go after our transports.

*Canberra*, burning fiercely, listing, unable to steam, and abandoned, was sunk by U.S. destroyer gunfire and torpedoes, and slipped below the waves at 0800 on the morning of 9 August 1942. She now rests upright at a depth of 2,500 feet, having been found in Iron Bottom Sound by Robert Ballard in 1992.

# "The *Helena* Doesn't Answer"

## CMDR. BILL BARNETT, USN (RET.)

*Commander Bill Barnett was born and raised in California. He entered the U.S. Naval Academy in 1938, and graduated in 1941, just in time to participate in some of the early fighting in the Pacific during World War II. He and his shipmates saw action throughout much of the Guadalcanal campaign at a time when the Japanese navy had the upper hand and was sinking Allied ships when few of them could be replaced. Having survived the sinking of the* Helena, *Barnett went on to serve for one year as a gunnery officer on the USS* Bataan, *a light carrier, then on the USS* Chevalier, *a destroyer. After the war, he served mostly on destroyers, and retired as a full commander in 1964. He now lives in Vacaville, California.*

At the Naval Academy I was taking my final exams on 7 December 1941, when the Japanese attacked Pearl Harbor. We graduated on 19 December 1941, and Frank Knox, the secretary of the navy, was the speaker at our graduation. He had just returned from Pearl Harbor. He spoke of the horrors he had seen there and how it was our job to go out and correct the situation. It was a very interesting talk. Anyway, after graduation me and three other classmates, Jimmy Salassi, Micky Riley, and Ray Casten, were assigned to the USS *Helena*. Later on, we were joined by Jack Ebnet, who was also a classmate. Jack had been on the USS *Chicago* when it was sunk, and was then assigned to *Helena*.

We traveled by ship from the West Coast out to Hawaii. When we arrived, I was astounded to see most of the Pacific Fleet—all the old battleships—sitting on the bottom of Pearl Harbor. There was still oil all over the harbor. It was a mess.

We found out that our ship, *Helena*, had been hit in the forward engine room during the Japanese attack. Emergency repairs had been made there at Pearl, and then she was sent back to Mare Island on the West Coast for more extensive repairs. We had to turn around and go to Mare Island to catch the ship. I was on *Helena* for eighteen months until she was sunk at the Battle of Kula Gulf.

I was placed in the gunnery department. All this new equipment was coming aboard. Five-inch/thirty-eight twin antiaircraft dual purpose mounts, 40-mm, and 20-mm guns were spread throughout the ship. We also had two floatplanes that we carried on the after part of the ship, along with the two catapults for launching them. They were for scouting out the enemy.

We left Mare Island after all repairs were made and headed out for the South Pacific. We arrived at this base called Espiritu Santo, which was in the New Hebrides. We operated out of that base the whole time we were down there for the campaign in the Solomon Islands. We were with the USS *Wasp*, a carrier, when she was sunk just north of the Coral Sea on 15 September 1942. She was torpedoed by a Japanese submarine and was so heavily damaged that our own destroyers had to sink her. The battleship *North Carolina* took a torpedo that day too, but kept on going over the horizon at about 32 knots.

There were four other cruisers that were sunk in the naval battles for Guadalcanal before we got into the fight, *Vincennes, Canberra, Astoria,* and *Quincy,* As a result, we were sort of stuck there with just some destroyers and cruisers *Honolulu, St. Louis,* and *San Francisco.* That destroyer squadron and those cruisers were our task force in the Solomons.

I remember one officer, Warren Boles. He was in the main battery. Warren was rather rough-hewn, tall and angular, but a fearless guy. He was the type of individual you need in a war, because he enjoyed combat. All he wanted to do was kill Japs.

We got into several battles in support of our troops there on Guadalcanal. Once, the Japanese attacked us with about sixteen torpedo bombers. We shot down most of them. I think *Helena* was credited with four. After that, we were heading back south when we got word that an entire Japanese task force was heading down the "Slot," so we turned around and headed back. That was 14–15 November 1942. We engaged the enemy and went in between two lines of Japanese ships. Several of our destroyers were lost. *San Francisco* was badly shot up, and Admirals Scott and Callaghan were killed during the fighting.

When we left the area the next morning, our captain, Gilbert C. Hoover, was the senior officer afloat, and all we had with us were *San Francisco* and *Juneau*, both cruisers. *Juneau* was the ship that the five Sullivan brothers were on.

We ran into trouble on the way back down the Slot. A Japanese submarine was tracking us, and it sank *Juneau*. I was on the after 40-mm guns and saw the torpedoes go right into *Juneau*. I could see a signalman on the bridge of *Juneau* with his semaphore flags when it was torpedoed. I don't know how many torpedoes hit her, but they blew that ship to smithereens. The guy with the semaphore flags was lifted right into the air. It was a horrible sight, and when the smoke cleared there wasn't anything around. *Juneau* was gone!

We had two destroyers with us, and I think only one of them had sonar gear for hunting down the sub. So besides the two destroyers, we were left with just two cruisers. One was *San Francisco*, which was all shot up, and us. As it turned out, there were ten or twelve survivors from *Juneau*. However, at the time it didn't look like there were any survivors. Our captain, Gilbert C. Hoover, who, like I said, was the senior officer afloat, decided it was best to save the ships that were left. We proceeded from the area, thinking other ships would be sent out later if there were any survivors. As it turned out, there were survivors and there was a big hullabaloo about that, and Admiral Halsey summarily relieved our captain for leaving the scene. The Navy Department later exonerated him, but his career was ruined. He should have made admiral, but never made it past captain until he retired. He retired as a rear admiral—what they call a "tombstone" promotion.

For us of *Helena*, this was a terrible thing, because Captain Hoover was loved by every man aboard. He was a wonderful captain. He had come to us from a destroyer squadron where he had won a Navy Cross and other decorations for heroism. We were devastated by the fact that he had to leave us. But another officer, Capt. Charles P. Cecil, replaced him.

Sometime after that, we were sent down to Sydney, Australia, for rest and recuperation, and to go into dry dock to have the bottom of the ship cleaned and get needed engine repairs. We spent about a month in Australia, then went back into combat in the Solomons, which included bombardment of Japanese shore positions. That is when we got into the battle where we were sunk—the Battle of Kula Gulf. By that time Guadalcanal was pretty well secured, but the Japanese were on the island of Munda, as well as other islands to the north, and they were reinforcing them. Kula Gulf was right between New Georgia Island and Kolombangara Island, and the Japanese were using these islands as staging points. That is in the area where the Battle of Kula Gulf took place.

I was on the fighting bridge the night we were sunk. The Japanese made a destroyer torpedo attack against us. Their torpedoes missed *Honolulu*, which was ahead of us, and hit *Helena*. The first torpedo hit our bow and knocked it off up to the second gun turret. Everybody in the forward turret was killed. One of my best friends was in that turret. His name was Swede Hansen. I was fortunate to meet his mother and father years later, when I was working at the Pentagon. I told them what I knew about their son, how he was lost that night, and how I felt about him as a friend and shipmate. I think that brought some comfort to them.

A second and third torpedo hit us amidships, breaking the keel. The last two people to leave the bridge were me and my assistant, Ozzie Koerner. The captain had left, and the gunnery officer had left, so we figured we had better leave too. A radio antenna fell on the bridge and hit our communications officer, Vic Post, who was with the captain at the time. Me and another guy pulled that off him, then we went down to the quarterdeck and found ourselves hip-deep in water. The ship was already going down, so I just swam off.

I was a pretty good swimmer in those days, so I didn't climb into a raft, but eventually hung on to one of them. We were in the water quite a while and were wondering what was going to happen to us, whether we were going to become prisoners of the Japanese, or whether we were going to be rescued by one of our ships. Then I saw some ships come back. They were destroyers, but at the time we didn't know if they were Japanese or ours. When they got close we saw that they had cargo nets over the sides, so we knew they were retrieving survivors. They didn't stop for long while picking us up because there was still the possibility of enemy ships in the area, and they didn't want to be sunk too. The USS *Radford* was the one that picked me up. As a matter of fact, I made a model of it and my assistant, Ozzie Koerner, named his first son after *Radford*.

**Survivors of USS *Helena*, a cruiser sunk during the Battle of Kula Gulf in the Solomon Islands.**

We were all covered with fuel oil, and general quarters was sounded a couple of times while we were on board, so we had to get under cover and out of the way of the guns. We cleaned some of the fuel oil off with diesel oil. Diesel oil will cut crude oil.

The chief engineer of *Helena*, Cmdr. Elmer C. Buerkle, got sucked into the propellers of the destroyer and was killed. I don't know how many others were killed in the water that night. Actually, we had a remarkable number of survivors. We had over 1,100 men aboard and I don't know how many survived, but a good proportion of them did.

*Radford* took us to Tulagi and transferred us to one of the cruisers. I think it was *St. Louis,* and from there we were taken to Espiritu Santo.

Not all the survivors were rescued by the destroyers that night. Some of them swam or paddled to a small island called Vella Lavella. They had lots of problems. There were Japanese on that island, but the natives were not friendly with them. I guess the Japanese didn't treat the natives well, so the natives took care of the survivors and moved them out of the way of Japanese patrols in the area until they could be rescued. I think if the survivors hadn't been rescued, in time the Japanese would most likely have found them and killed them.

Captain Cecil wasn't in survivors' camp with us. He was transferred someplace else right away. I never saw him after that. I know he made admiral. However, he was later killed, and a destroyer was named after him.

You know, we were all so young then. We had eighteen, nineteen, twenty-year-old kids in the crew. Now, we get together every two years and talk about old times and realize we are a bunch of old men.

# Aboard the USS *Zane*, DMS-14

## CAPT. JOSEPH B. DRACHNIK, USN (RET.)

*Captain Joseph B. Drachnik was born in Ross, California, but spent most of his early life in Brown's Valley, near Vacaville, California. In spite of family financial difficulties, Drachnik did well in school. He was a star athlete and was elected class president and later student body president at Vacaville Union High School. He attended the University of California at Berkeley for a couple of years, but transferred at the end of his sophomore year to the U.S. Naval Academy. He graduated from the Academy in 1942 and left to his first duty assignment aboard the USS* Zane, *DMS-14. His older brother, a spotting pilot in the Army Coast Artillery, was killed in the Philippines during the last year of the war. After thirty years of service, Drachnik retired from the navy in 1972. He lives in Sacramento, California. The USS* Zane, *DD-337, was commissioned in 1921. In 1940 it was reclassified as DMS-14, destroyer minesweeper. It survived the Japanese attack on Pearl Harbor on 7 December 1941, as well as several other major engagements during the war. In June 1945 the* Zane *was converted once again, this time to a miscellaneous auxiliary, AG-109. In December of that year,* Zane *was decommissioned. In 1946* Zane *was struck from the list of navy ships, and scrapped in 1947. It had six battle stars and the Navy Unit Commendation before it was no more.*

When I graduated from Vacaville Union High School in June 1937, I was determined to go to college. Those were the Depression years and everybody was poverty-stricken, but those who were the most poverty-stricken were those who had no particular occupation in life.

114

I hitchhiked down to Berkeley with the $35 I had in my pocket from picking apricots at twenty cents an hour. I spent a couple of years at the University of California, working my way through. Things were getting tighter and tighter, and I was finding that I could not keep my grades up and work too. So I figured I had to find some other way to get ahead.

One summer, I was working on my congressman's fruit ranch. His name was Frank Buck, and his fruit ranch was in Vacaville. The foreman said, "Young man, if I were you I would hit up the old man for an appointment to one of the military academies." I had never thought of that. I went back to Cal and struggled along for another few months. Then one day I was in the campus barber

Capt. Joseph Drachnik, a graduate of the U.S. Naval Academy, Class of '42. His first sea duty was aboard USS *Zane*, DMS-14, an old four-stack destroyer converted to mine sweeping. His replacement aboard *Zane* later in the war was Herman Wouk, author of *The Caine Mutiny*.

shop and saw a three-inch headline in the *San Francisco Examiner*: "HITLER INVADES POLAND." It was obvious to me that we would be in the war before long. Sometime after that, I read a notice that Mr. Buck was sponsoring a competitive examination for an appointment to the Naval Academy. I rode a bus to Vallejo and took the exam with about 130 other people.

In February 1939, I received a special delivery letter from my congressman, saying he had an appointment to the Naval Academy for me, and to wire him if I wanted it. I had to borrow fifty cents from my brother in order to send a telegram saying I accepted the appointment.

One of the proudest days in my life was when I was voted student body president at Vacaville Union High School. When I got to the Naval Academy, guess what? Every one of the 680 fellows who entered the

Academy that year had been presidents of their student bodies, captains of their football teams, and all the other things that went on back at their high schools. In other words, the competition was pretty stiff. Perhaps that is why we are the only class in the history of the Academy to have had two chiefs of naval operations from the same class. One was Elmo Zumwalt and the other was Jim Holloway.

Three years later we graduated. At the beginning of our third year at the Naval Academy our classes were compressed. All the fun stuff, like the summer cruise, was cut out and we graduated in June 1942 instead of 1943. After graduation, we had a couple of weeks of leave, then reported for duty. My ship, and those of many of my classmates, was based in Pearl Harbor. I sailed from San Francisco on a transport, the USS *Zeilin*, I believe it was, with about sixty of my classmates on 6 July 1942.

My ship, the USS *Zane*, DMS-14, was a destroyer-minesweeper. She was a converted World War I destroyer, formerly DD-337 that had had one boiler removed and minesweeping gear installed. She was supposed to be in Pearl Harbor, but when we got there she was gone. The fleet had sailed for parts unknown, and nobody would say where. This was the early part of the war; ship movements were secret, and secrets were closely guarded.

After a couple of weeks at the bachelors officers' quarters at Pearl, I received two sets of orders on the same day. One set directed me to report to the base commander for duty on a harbor oiler. A couple of hours later I received a message from Washington to board a transport, the USS *Betelgeuse*, for transportation to *Zane*. I thought that sounded a lot better than hanging around Pearl Harbor, so I reported aboard the transport. When we sailed the next morning we had no idea where we were going. Nobody would tell us.

After some three weeks at sea we found ourselves somewhere down near the Coral Sea. We were asked to attend an intelligence briefing. There, we learned that elements of the First Marine Division that were also aboard were going to invade Guadalcanal, an island in the Solomon group. An article in the *National Geographic*, by Osa Johnson, a well-known explorer of out-of-the-way places, was the basis of about all we knew about Guadalcanal at the time.

On 5 August 1942, we woke up to see an ocean of masts on the horizon. Here were most of the ships of the United States Pacific Fleet, ready to invade Guadalcanal. We were embarked in Higgins boats and transferred to our ships. My ship, *Zane*, had been in the Pacific for some time and was badly in need of a paint job. She had rust streaks all over her. She didn't look very imposing to me.

Nonetheless, our skipper was one of the finest captains I ever served under during my military career, and it was good to serve under a man like him on my very first tour of duty. His name was Lt. Cmdr. Peyton L. Wirtz, class of 1931—a really memorable guy, in my opinion. He would spend innumerable hours, thirty-six hours at a stretch on the bridge with little sleep, making sure everything was under control. Of course, most of the rest of us were up a good part of that time, too, at general quarters, fighting off air attacks, or on alert.

The crew was made up of experienced men. Most of them were career men, not Johnny-come-lately draftees. We had a few Filipinos aboard. They were mostly stewards in those days. However, we did have a Filipino who was on the deck force. I understand he was sixty years old, but he looked thirty. We also had a black chief steward, who managed the wardroom pantry. He was a big, husky fellow, and whenever we went to general quarters he hung a meat ax in his belt. We used to think, "God help any Jap he might come across." I might also add that nobody ever raided his pantry.

*Zane* already had a full complement of officers, so they welded a bunk to the bulkhead for me in the wardroom, which I didn't see much of anyway, since I was on watch or at general quarters most of the time I was aboard.

A day and a half later, on 7 August 1942, we invaded Guadalcanal. Our mission was to shell the hills around the harbor and minesweep the approaches to Tulagi Harbor. The Japanese retaliated on the eighth with an air raid. We were alerted to it by coast watchers—Australian guys who were situated clandestinely on islands to the north. We would get a warning message of aircraft heading our way, and the fleet would get underway, so as not to get caught there like sitting ducks. These Japanese bombers were twin-engine planes called "Bettys," and they came over in "V" formations. They were very high, but visibility down there was amazingly clear—bright, beautiful days, with cumulus clouds. You could see forever.

On this day our fighters took care of the enemy escorts—the Zeros—and that left the Bettys with no protection, so they came down to the surface. We had one coming straight at us. My battle station was the after

gun mount. We had a 3-inch .50-caliber and a 20-mm, and that Betty
was headed right for me. I was looking down the gun barrels on its wings,
and I could clearly see the two pilots. That plane was so low to the water
that the pilots were almost at eye level with me. As the plane went by
our starboard quarter, our 20-mm cut his tail off. It didn't crash—it
ditched. What followed, I didn't see personally, because I was busy back
aft. But when this Jap ditched, our captain decided it would be a good
thing to salvage the plane and take the crew prisoner, so he headed the
ship over to it. Meanwhile, one of the pilots crawled out on to the wing
and was standing there with his arms folded. The ship pulled up to him,
with our people yelling at him to come aboard. He pulled out a pistol
and started shooting at our people on the bridge, so one of our 20-mm
guns opened up, cutting him to pieces and sinking the airplane. That
was the closest I ever got to any Japs during the war.

That night, after the air attack, we were patrolling off Lunga Point.
Lunga Point is the beach where we had put the marines ashore on
Guadalcanal. I had the mid-watch. Sometime after midnight, we saw
flashes and heard the thunder of guns to the northeast. We were about
ten miles from where the Battle of Savo Island was taking place. I was
out on the wing of the bridge when the captain came over and said to
me, "Ensign Drachnik, I think it's an amazing coincidence for a young
officer on one of his first watches of his navy career to be in the middle
of a sea battle." I didn't have much of a rejoinder. I said something like,
"Well, it's more fun than classes back at the Naval Academy were."

We spent the next year in and out of the Guadalcanal area, either
there or en route to Espiritu Santo or Noumea. We seemed to arrive at
the same time or within a couple of days of every major battle that
occurred there. We would always see airplane wheels, life rafts, and the
like, floating around as we came into the area.

Our navy was stretched very thin at that time. The U.S. had had
eighteen heavy cruisers in the Pacific when the war started. By October
1942, six of them had been sunk, six had been badly damaged, and we
only had six operational ones left, plus a couple of carriers. The modern
destroyers we had were used mostly as escorts for the carriers. So they
used *Zane*, and the few other ships like us, for just about everything else.

We used to run from Guadalcanal back to Espiritu Santo, which was
our forward base southeast of Guadalcanal. I don't remember how far
away it was—maybe 500 miles. We carried deckloads of aviation torpedoes

and drums of aviation gasoline for the marine aircraft on Henderson Field. It was pretty hairy business, because if a bomb hit within a hundred yards of us we probably would have gone up in smoke.

On 25 August we were about to leave Tulagi Harbor. We had taken up another load of torpedoes to the PT boat squadrons that were then based on Tulagi, when we were asked by General Vandegrift of the marines to stand by to do some shore bombardment in the afternoon. At about ten o'clock in the morning three Japanese destroyers were sighted coming over the horizon. There were two ships in our formation. The other ship was the USS *Trevor*, DMS-16. The captain of the *Trevor* was the senior captain, and therefore the officer in tactical command. He opted to make a run for it. We were two very old destroyers. The Jap ships were new destroyers. They had 4.7-inch guns. We had 3-inch guns. The maximum range of our guns was 13,000 yards. Theirs could shoot 15,000 yards, and the enemy ships had greater speed. Our maximum speed was twenty-seven knots. The Japanese destroyer could probably make between thirty-two and thirty-five knots, so we high-tailed it out of there and headed for Sealark Channel.

We had a running gun battle for the next forty minutes. I was now in the engineering department, and my battle station at this point was in the forward boiler room, so I didn't see what was going on, which was probably just as well. I sat down there saying my rosaries and thinking about what might happen if a shell came through the bulkhead.

These Japanese were very good gunners, but they made the mistake of aligning their guns so well that the shells landed very close together, in a very tight pattern. What you want to do is align the guns so that when the shells land they cover a fifty or a hundred-yard area. That way, during the flight of the shells the target can't get out from under the pattern. The Japs were firing their patterns so tight that the shells were landing within a few yards of each other. When one of their salvos landed we would turn and the next salvo would land where we were. Still, we took more than a few straddles. We were at an extreme range, and their shells were coming down at such a sharp angle that they took down all of our halyards, except the one holding the American flag. The shells came down through the rigging, missing the ship and hitting the water. However, one shell did hit our 3-inch gun, right on the elevation handwheel of the gun pointer, killing four or five men.

At that point, and just when we thought we were done for, the Japs broke off their attack. They then went over to Lunga Point and sank a fleet tug, *Seminole*.

Henderson Field, on Guadalcanal, had recently been bombed and was a muddy mess. When planes were finally able to get off the ground, they reported one of the Jap destroyers on fire, and we were given credit for having gotten hits on it. That was amazing because the range was extreme for our guns. Fortunately, we had a doctor on board. After we were hit, I was appointed anesthesiologist, probably because I was the junior officer. On a destroyer, the wardroom table becomes an operating room table. The fellow we were treating was our boatswain's mate, the surviving gun captain of the gun that was hit. A one-inch chunk of bone had been torn from his shin by shrapnel. The doctor handed me a small strainer with a piece of gauze in it, and a can of ether. The man was a burly young fellow, and it took two and a half cans of ether to put him under. He lived, and was shipped off to a hospital when we reached port. We never saw him again after that.

On some of those trips we would anchor in Tulagi Harbor and I would visit some of my naval academy classmates who were with the PT squadron based there. They had been issued army tents, but had traded those to the local natives in exchange for use of their village as an encampment. The natives went happily off and lived in the tents.

In February 1943, we were sent off to land a meteorological party on a small island called Anuda, or Cherry Island, in the Santa Cruz group. Anuda was interesting in that it was such a primitive place—exactly what you would see in movies of the South Pacific. We anchored about a quarter-mile from a sandy beach and the natives came out in outrigger canoes. Some even swam out to the ship. So here we had these natives aboard, looking like cannibals, with their loincloths and woven hats. One was the chief. He knew a little English and we were able to communicate with him a bit. The primary question we had for him was, "Are there any Japs on the island?" He indicated that there weren't any. Then he pointed to our flag and said, "Good, good."

We had a difficult time there because the only transportation we had was our whaleboats. The weather was bad and there was a heavy surf. In landing the party, both whaleboats broached in the surf. We finally got the group's meteorological gear and other supplies ashore on life rafts and native canoes, but we had to leave some of our own men ashore to be picked up later.

In the latter part of February, our forces began moving up the line and landing on islands to the northwest. The first was Russell Island, a few hours' run from Tulagi. A battalion of army troops had been put ashore there by heavy landing craft that had made the voyage from Guadalcanal. A day or so later, we and another destroyer-minesweeper embarked two companies of army troops and proceeded stealthily at night to the site. We lay to in a little cove about midnight and tried to contact the battalion on shore, but without success. We didn't know whether the Japs had wiped out the battalion or what. We had towed a landing craft up with us for landing the troops. Again I was on the mid-watch, and the captain said to me, "Joe, get in the boat and go with them as boat officer." The recognition signal was supposed to be three flashes on a red flashlight, and the answer back was to be the same three flashes. We went in slowly, cut the engines some ways off the beach, and I gave the signal. No answer!

An army second lieutenant was in charge of the company, and the two of us held a council of war and decided since we could see a quad 40-mm gun mount at the edge of the beach, and we weren't being shot at, the least we could do was go in and see what was going on. We quietly pulled up to the beach, dropped the ramp, and debarked the troops. The troops found the troops manning the gun. They were Americans and they were sound asleep.

Everything seemed fine. I took the boat back to the ship, and the ship went back to Guadalcanal. I was sound asleep when, at seven o'clock in the morning, a messenger woke me up and said, "The admiral wants to see you over on Guadalcanal." The admiral was Admiral Turner, and Admiral Turner, as COMSOPAC (Commander South Pacific Forces), was commander of all naval operations in the theatre.

There was a PT boat waiting alongside the ship for me. I jumped in and we charged across the twenty miles or so of channel at thirty-five knots. On the other side was a jeep waiting for me, and it took me through the jungle on a very muddy track. We reached a group of canvas tents with wooden floors and wood sides about three or four feet high—the admiral's headquarters. The admiral's chief of staff asked me if I had had anything to eat. I had not, so he took me to the mess tent and I had my first steak in months. The army was eating better than the navy. I was then taken in to see Admiral Turner. He wanted to know just what had happened the night before. The problem was, there had been

no communication from the battalion that had been landed on Russell
Island. The commander didn't know if the battalion had been overrun
by Japs, or what. I was the only person who had been there and knew
anything. I thought that was one of my greatest moments. Here was one
of the people running the war and he wanted to know from me what
was going on.

In March 1943, we escorted the USS *Portland* and some transports
from Guadalcanal to New Zealand. *Portland* had been torpedoed and was
missing part of its bow or stern, I don't remember which. On the way,
we ran into a typhoon, which was the worst weather I have ever seen in
my thirty-year career in the navy. It was so rough you had to look up at
about a thirty-degree angle to see the crests of the waves. The sea was
totally green, and the spray was blowing in horizontal streaks. Just as we
thought we were going to be inundated by a wave, the ship would shud-
der and chug its way up it and down the other side. In the middle of the
night our depth charge racks started coming apart. Adding to all the other
confusion, our depth charges began rolling over the stern and detonating
close aboard.

About that time, we lost steering control. The communications from
the bridge to steering went out, so they sent me and the first lieutenant
back to the steering engine compartment, a cramped space about six feet
wide and eight feet long, with the steering engine in the middle of it and
hardly enough room for us to move. We received steering orders by
sound-powered telephone and manually operated the steering engine.
We were in the very stern of the ship, being tossed around by a very bad
storm, and it really wasn't much fun. Control from the bridge was restored
after a couple of hours, and we made it to Auckland without any loss of
life.

On 30 June 1943, we were back in the Solomons. *Zane* and the USS
*Talbot*, APD-7, embarked a company of army troops. Our mission was
to land them on the next island up the chain, an island near Munda where
the Japanese had an airfield. This was just before the invasion of Munda,
scheduled for the following day. We were to land our troops on an island
named Ndume, near a village called Sasavele. While we were landing the
troops at 3:00 o'clock in the morning, the ship ran aground. We backed
off, but right into a coral head and bent our screws. So there we were
dead in the water. We jettisoned our anchor and some other stuff but
couldn't break free. Some hours later, a fleet tug arrived and towed us back

to Guadalcanal. By then, the landings on Munda had been completed, and we joined up with the invasion force returning to Guadalcanal. On the way back we came under air attack by a significant number of Jap planes. We got through that all right, but Admiral Turner's flagship, the USS *McCawley*, an amphibious command ship, was damaged. The ship had to be abandoned, but plans were to go back the next day and salvage it. However, the PT boats had been told that after the landings there would be no U.S. ships left in the area, so when they sighted *McCawley* that night, they torpedoed and sank it.

In early July 1943, my relief reported aboard. His name was Ensign Herman Wouk, who later rose to fame with his book *The Caine Mutiny*. I haven't seen him since, but the crew of *Zane* has an active association and I understand he attended one of the reunions a few years ago.

We received some emergency repairs at Espiritu Santo, and then on 1 August 1943 started on the long voyage home on one screw, in company with the cruiser USS *St. Louis*. She had had her bow blown off by a torpedo.

We arrived at Mare Island Naval Shipyard on 19 August 1943, and shortly thereafter I left the USS *Zane* for duty on a new destroyer, the USS *Allen M. Sumner*, DD-692, the titular ship of the new Sumner Class, with twin-mount five-inch guns.

One of *Zane's* sailors, Sonarman Joseph Gunterman, was successful in real estate after the war. In the early 1990s, he visited Sasavele Village on Ndume Island where *Zane* had jettisoned her anchor. He found the natives had raised it and had it up on the beach. The people of the village remembered *Zane* and what had happened there during World War II. Mr. Gunterman supplied the funds, and a memorial was constructed there around the anchor, with a plaque commemorating our adventure. Also, *Zane's* ship's bell is now in a church steeple in San Juan Capistrano, California.

During the period of these adventures, I knew little about what was going on back home. I had been cooped up in the Naval Academy for three years. I graduated, and two weeks later I was on my way to Guadalcanal. I last saw my mother on graduation day at the academy. I saw my brother, who had been off on an army exercise in Oregon, just before we sailed from San Francisco in July 1942. Before I could get home my mother learned of my brother's death in the Philippines and dropped dead of an apparent heart attack.

> "It's a scary feeling when you hear these guns going
> off and you know the kamikaze is getting closer and
> closer but you can't see anything; then he hits."

# Aboard the USS *Long*, DMS-12

## Benjamin F. Cator

*Mr. Cator was born in Los Angeles, California, in 1918, but lived in the
San Francisco Bay Area until after the war, when he moved to Sacramento,
California. When the Japanese bombed Pearl Harbor he was in his senior year at Oregon State College. He volunteered for the navy's V-7 program, and upon graduation was sent to Columbia University for officer
training. Three months later he graduated and was commissioned an ensign
in the U.S. Navy. After thirty days' leave he reported aboard USS* Long,
DD-209, *which at the time was in Kodiak, Alaska. The* Long *was commissioned in 1919. In November 1940, it was converted to a destroyer-
minesweeper, DMS-12. Cator, on board* Long, *participated in the U.S.
efforts to retake the Aleutian islands of Attu and Kiska from the Japanese.
Following a stint in dry dock at Mare Island, California,* Long *went west
to sweep mines in the central and southwest Pacific.* Long, *like a number
of other fast minesweepers, did not survive the war. Mr. Cator did, and is
retired and living in Sacramento, California.*

    In early March 1944, we got orders to help with the landings in the
Admiralty Islands—Los Negros and Manus. It was our job to sweep a
channel into Seeadler Harbor, which was a big harbor at Manus Island.
The channel we had to sweep was between some smaller islands, and *Long*
and several other destroyer-minesweepers streamed out their sweep gear
and attempted to enter the channel when we were repulsed by enemy gunfire coming from these small islands. We returned fire, but still couldn't
enter the channel to sweep for mines because of the enemy fire. It would
have been suicide.

Some of our destroyers bombarded the islands, and then we tried entering the channel again. The enemy guns were still not knocked out, so we had to delay our sweep for several days while some of our cruisers came up and silenced the enemy guns. Finally, we did enter the channel and swept. We swept some magnetic mines that had been laid by Australian PBYs a number of weeks earlier, and that was it. That was the only time we ever swept any magnetic mines.

There were three types of mines used during World War II, and there were three ways of sweeping. There were magnetic mines, moored mines, and acoustic mines. Most of the sweeping was for moored mines. In sweeping for moored mines there were usually two ships sweeping together in formation, depending on the size of the area. Each ship had two paravanes, one on each side of the stern. They would be streamed out behind the ship several hundred feet. There were serrated cables that connected the ship to the vanes, and the cables were depressed under the water so that if the cables hit the cable of a moored mine, it cut it just by running it along the serrated edges. If the serrated cable didn't cut the mine from its mooring cable, there was a cutter at the end of the paravane, and the mine would bob up to the surface. Then it was up to the ship or a mine disposal ship to detonate it by gunfire.

For acoustic mines we streamed from the side of the ship with a bunch of metal bars that made a terrific racket and that would set them off. This way we could stream for both moored and acoustic mines at the same time. However, we never did encounter any acoustic mines during the time I was aboard.

You couldn't sweep for moored mines and magnetic mines at the same time. For magnetic mines we strung two long cables behind the ship with an electric current jumping back and forth between the two at their ends. This would create a pulse that would set these magnetic mines off. Of course, magnetic mines were set to go off under the second, third, fourth, or fifth ship to go over them. And also, all of our ships were what they called "degaussed." We would go into a degaussing station like the one at Pearl Harbor where all these cables were wrapped around the ship and electric current was run through them. This supposedly took away the magnetic field from the ship so we wouldn't set off magnetic mines. Of course, the only time we ran into magnetic mines was during the sweep we did of Seeadler Channel.

It was shortly after our operations in the Admiralty Islands that we received orders to participate in the landings at Hollandia, which was on the north coast of New Guinea. That was in April 1944. Two minesweepers, *Long* and *Hogan,* DMS-6, entered Humboldt Harbor before the invasion and swept the harbor. While we were going in I remember the captain saying, "Fire on anything you see!" We went in firing all of our guns, but we didn't receive any return fire. It turns out that when the Japs saw all the activity they pulled back into the mountains. We swept the harbor and no mines were found. Later that day the transports entered and the troops made their landings.

After the landings at Hollandia we set out for Eniwetok Atoll to prepare for the landings at Saipan. Eniwetok is a huge atoll. There were hundreds and hundreds of ships in there. You could see masts sticking up over the horizon.

We were the first ships to leave for Saipan on 10 June 1944. There were ten destroyer-minesweepers that sortied that day. We arrived off Saipan on the thirteenth and started sweeping the transport area. We swept there for several days, but no mines were found. We were never fired on by the Japanese while we were sweeping. I guess they didn't want to give away their gun positions.

After we were done sweeping for mines we gave fire support for some underwater demolition teams that were going in close to the beach, looking for underwater obstacles. They went in during the daytime, and they went in real close. Some of those guys went almost onto the beach. They were fired on, and several were killed. I remember one of them being lifted from a rubber boat into an APD.

After the transports and other ships arrived we were put on anti-submarine patrol. Quite a few Japanese planes came over while we were out there. One came up our starboard side, low to the water, and was not detected by our radar. He came by us and waved; he was that close. Before we could bring our guns to bear on him he was gone. He wasn't interested in us. He was going in for bigger stuff.

After that, another Jap plane was shot down near us by one of our fighters, and the pilot bailed out. As he was coming down in his parachute, we steamed over to pick him up. But when he saw us coming over, he cut himself loose from his parachute and dropped into the water to his death.

Prior to the invasion of Tinian, we did an exploratory sweep for mines between Tinian and Saipan. We didn't find any mines, but while we were off the beach, one of our fliers was shot down by antiaircraft fire from Tinian. He ditched fairly close to the beach, so we launched our whaleboat. With several men in the whaleboat, we went in to pick up the pilot, but about halfway there the engine in the whaleboat conked out. We could see bullets hitting the water around us. So then the ship launched the captain's gig. It came in, picked us up, went in and picked the flier up, then came back and towed the whaleboat back to the ship.

We also had some escort carriers there at Saipan. They brought in a bunch of P-47s to be launched as soon as the airfield on Saipan was secured. The P-47 resembles, to some extent, a Zero, and when they were launched and came in to land on Saipan just about every ship in the fleet opened up on them, thinking they were Japanese. Although none of them were shot down, you could hear the command ship over the radio, "Stop firing! Stop firing! They are friendlies!"

We changed the position of our antisubmarine patrols several times there off Saipan, and one time we came across some Japanese bodies in the water. We heard later that a lot of Japanese had committed suicide by jumping off the cliffs of Saipan into the water.

After the landings at Guam we pulled out and went down to Espiritu Santo in the New Hebrides, then up to Florida Island near Guadalcanal. From there, forty-three minesweepers left the Solomons for Palau on 6 September 1944.

We did a pre-invasion sweep between Peleliu and Angaur. There were many mines in this area. One of the minesweepers, the USS *Perry*, another DMS, hit a mine and sank. The survivors were rescued by another ship just before she went down.

When the marines landed several days later, we moved up to Kossol Passage, which was at the north end of the big island, Babeldaop. There were lots of mines in there too, and we swept for several days because the navy wanted to use that area as an anchorage for the bigger ships. The water was so clear there we could actually see the mines as we went over them. In many instances we could see the mines before we had a chance to sweep them.

After the Palau landings, we grouped up at Manus Island in the Admiralties for the landings at Leyte in the Philippines. We sortied out of Manus on 10 October 1944. There were probably eighty or ninety minesweepers that went up in one group with maybe one destroyer. We had YMSs, which were small wooden minesweepers, and AMs, which were bigger metal minesweepers, and the DMSs, which were the destroyer-minesweepers. The YMSs and AMs did most of the close-in sweepings. The ones that usually went in before the landings were the DMSs; they were considered fast minesweepers. They would sweep the transport area, and sweep areas for the bombardment ships so they could get in and be safe from mines.

It was 1,500 miles up to Leyte, and we were going at nine knots, so it took us a long time to make it. When we got up to the Philippines the weather got real rough. We started sweeping on 17 October and the invasion was scheduled for 20 October. The problem was there were a lot of mines, but we couldn't detonate them. We swept them, and they floated to the surface, but it was so stormy and windy that very few of them were detonated. The result was, there were a lot of mines floating around.

We swept a forty-five-mile channel up Leyte Gulf and led the transports up that night with our sweeping gear out. When the troops landed on the twentieth, the weather had calmed down and we spent one whole day just detonating floating mines. And of course, our main concern was hitting one at night. However, no one hit one, which was fortunate.

We anchored in the transport area at night and there were quite a few Jap planes that came over in the evening about sunset, and all the ships would start making smoke at about five o'clock in the evening. That smoke would completely envelop the whole transport area so that from above you couldn't see any of the ships. At least that was the idea.

The landings were on 20 October, and on 23 October we left there with a group of empty transports. We left the day before the Battle of Surigao Strait, which was a classic naval battle between surface ships. We formed up again at Manus for the landings at Lingayen Gulf on the island of Luzon. There were hundreds of ships there at Manus in Seeadler Harbor. While at anchor, I was on deck just looking at all these ships, when all of a sudden one of them blew up! It literally disintegrated! It was *Mt. Hood*, which was an ammunition ship. We weren't close enough to have any damage done to us, but several ships that were tied up alongside of her were also sunk, and others were damaged. Nobody ever found out what caused it to blow up. Everybody from that ship was killed except a work party that was on the beach.

We departed 23 December 1944 for Leyte Gulf. We picked up some more minesweepers there and headed out through Surigao Strait into the Sulu Sea, then north to Lingayen Gulf, off Luzon. There were approximately one hundred ships in this convoy, most of them minesweepers. Except for a destroyer and an Australian corvette, our only support was about one hundred miles behind us in the form of some escort carriers, old battleships, and some cruisers and destroyers. They gave us some air cover and that was about it.

After we left Leyte, we had one suicide plane attack us near Mindanao on 3 January. It was a Jap Val and it hit the oiler *Cowanesque*, killing two men, but did little damage otherwise.

On 5 January we had nine separate kamikaze attacks on the convoy before we reached Lingayen Gulf that night. One or two of the YMSs were hit. Aside from the destroyer, we were the biggest ships in that convoy.

The next day, on 6 January 1945 at 7:30 that morning, before we started our sweep, a Jap plane dropped a bomb real close to our ship. Shortly after that, a suicide plane crashed close to us. Then another plane dropped two bombs that straddled us, and another suicide plane just missed our mast and crashed in the water. So before we even got started that morning we had all sorts of action.

We started to sweep up Lingayen Gulf, which was thirty-seven miles long. There were about four or five of us DMSs making these sweeps. We made one sweep up the gulf and back, then turned around for our second pass, and that is when we ran into more problems. At 12:10 P.M. that day, a lone Japanese plane crossed ahead of our formation low to the water. I was OOD—officer of the deck—at the time. Captain Caplan was also on the bridge, of course, and we were at general quarters. The plane made a turn and it didn't take long for us to see the kamikaze was coming right for us. We were firing everything we had at her, but she just kept coming.

I was on the port wing of the bridge, and just before she hit I walked through the wheelhouse and over to the starboard wing, but she didn't do any damage to the bridge. She hit us just below the bridge at the water line. She plowed into the wardroom and there were some casualties in the radio room just above the wardroom.

People on the bridge—the signalmen and radar people—dropped down onto the forecastle, leaving only the captain and me on the bridge. Then Captain Caplan left the bridge and went down on to the forecastle, and I ended up being the only person on the bridge. See, we had a fire on board and the forward magazine was below the bridge. The captain was afraid it was going to blow up.

The ship was dead in the water by then, so I dropped down onto the forecastle too. It was then that we decided to drop anchor and the captain gave the order to abandon ship. Well, it so happens that most of the crew on the back of the ship had already abandoned ship. We were eventually picked up by *Hovey*, DMS-10. She pulled in her sweep gear while the other ships continued with their sweep and came over and picked up most of the survivors. *Brooks*, which was an APD (destroyer-transport), picked up the rest.

I was on *Hovey* with the captain when he decided to send a salvage party over to *Long*, which had not yet sunk. The captain, the exec, and I, along with a salvage party, went aboard *Apache*, ATF-67. She was a fleet tug. It was getting dark, so we decided to spend the night on *Apache* and go over to *Long* the next morning. While we were on *Apache* she was attacked by a kamikaze, but it was shot down and crashed close aboard.

The next morning *Long* was still afloat, but low in the water. We went over in a whaleboat and came up on her stern. I went aboard with a couple of other guys, and as I walked forward the fantail started rising in the air. I ran back and jumped into the whaleboat, and as I did the stern of the ship rose into a vertical position and went right down. I pushed the whaleboat away on the propeller guard as she went down. She went down right beside us.

We went back to *Apache*, then transferred to the light cruiser *Columbia*. Early the next morning, before we transferred to *Columbia*, *Hovey* was hit by an aerial torpedo and sank. *Long* lost more men on *Hovey* than she did when she was hit by the kamikaze. *Hovey* lost quite a few of her people, too.

*Columbia* had been hit by kamikazes twice before I came aboard. There was a detachment of marines on board, and I befriended one of them. His general quarters position was up on what they called Sky-1, which was a director for the forward guns. The next day the troops were supposed to go ashore at Lingayen Gulf, and this Marine Corps officer said, "Why don't you come up with me on Sky-1. You get a hell of a view. You can see the bombardment of the beaches and the troops going in." I was going to go with him, and for some reason I didn't. And during the bombardment a suicide plane came in and hit Sky-1.

I was down in the wardroom when this happened. There were other survivors from *Long* down there, and we could hear the 5-inch guns going off. They were the long-range antiaircraft guns. And when they started going off you knew they were firing at a plane. Then the 40-mm guns would start firing, and you knew the plane had gotten closer. Then when the 20-mm guns started firing you knew the plane was real close. You should have seen those survivors of other kamikaze attacks; when those 20-mms started going off, they crawled under tables, behind chairs—they were trying to get any kind of protection they could find. Then the plane hit and the whole ship shook. It's a scary feeling when you hear these guns going off and you know the kamikaze is getting closer and closer but you can't see anything; then he hits.

*Columbia* had been hit three times by kamikazes. The Australian cruiser HMAS *Australia* had been hit four times by kamikazes. We formed up with the empty transports and pulled out of there and went back to Leyte Gulf. From there, we went on to Manus Island, where *Columbia* dropped us off.

After a few weeks on Manus the navy put all of us survivors on the USS *General Howze*, AP-134, a transport. When we arrived at the dock in San Francisco they had a band and everything there—a big welcoming crowd, because we were all survivors on this ship. Some were civilians who had been rescued from the Japanese. There were even some nuns, but mostly we were survivors from ships that had been sunk.

In April 1945, I received orders to report to the Naval Mine Warfare School in Yorktown, Virginia. I was there for sixty days as I recall, then I was assigned to the USS *Mervine*, another destroyer that was being converted to a minesweeper. After our trials we went down through the Panama Canal. While in the canal we received on board the operational plan for the invasion of Japan, and of course we wanted to see what our role was going to be, and it didn't look good. The plan told what to expect, and what we were going to do, and I don't think any of us felt we would come out of it alive. But before we got through the canal we received word about the dropping of the first atomic bomb, and before we got to San Diego they had dropped the second one, and the war was over.

# Aboard the USS *Charles Carroll,* APA-28

## LT. KENNETH BARDEN, USNR (RET.)

*Mr. Kenneth Barden was born in July 1923 in upstate New York. By
December 1942 he had had over a year of college, and had never seen the
ocean. His draft status was 1-A and he had to make a choice between going
into the service or getting a deferment for helping his father on the farm.
He chose the navy over the farm and applied for and was accepted into the
navy's V-12 program for reserve officers. Barden returned to civilian life
in 1946, but stayed in the Naval Reserve. He became an educator, first in
his native New York, then in California. Barden is now a retired teacher
and school administrator, but still active as a senior assemblyman in the
California State Legislature. He lives in Vallejo, California. The USS Charles
Carroll, APA-28 was originally launched as the SS Del Uruguay in 1942.
In August 1942 it was acquired by the U.S. Navy and commissioned the
USS Charles Carroll, AP-58. In February 1943 it was reclassified APA-
28, attack transport. Today it is part of the mothball fleet near San Fran-
cisco.*

In March 1944, after eight months in the V-12 program at Hobart
College in Geneva, New York, I was assigned to Midshipmen's School
in Plattsburgh, New York. I graduated from there in late June 1944, and
was commissioned an ensign in the United States Navy Reserve. I was
then sent to Fort Pierce, Florida, which was an amphibious boat base,
and completed my amphibious boat training there in December 1944.

Fort Pierce was a hellhole because we lived in tents and there were lots of mosquitoes and creepy-crawly things, but I learned a lot about small boat handling there. As a young ensign, I remember training an enlisted man—a coxswain. I was trying to teach him how to get a landing craft onto the beach and pull it back off. I kept giving him all these superfluous instructions, and finally he said, "Mr. Barden, if you will just shut up and leave me alone I think I can get this boat in and back off the beach without any problem." He did, and I realized then that I was over-instructing him.

The navy wanted me to stay there as an instructor, where I could have sat out the war if I had wanted to, but I didn't want to do that. My boat group, which had become very cohesive, was scheduled to go aboard the USS *Charles Carroll*, APA-28, an attack transport, which was at Norfolk, Virginia and had just returned from the European theatre. It was named after one of the signers of the Declaration of Independence. I declined the instructorship and went aboard *Carroll*, and eight days later sailed for the South Pacific by way of the Panama Canal.

Our first captain when I went aboard was Capt. Elliot Strauss. He was only on board for about ten months. He was replaced by a Captain Butterfield, a very bitter old man who had been in World War I and had been passed over for admiral and combat command as well. He was assigned to this attack transport, *Carroll*, and he wasn't very happy about it. He was a very indecisive man—always changing his mind. He was with us for about a year, then we had a Commander Thwing take over, who had been a reservist between the wars, and this was his first command. I think he was there when I left the ship in 1946. He was all right, but he didn't have good operational boat-handling skills like the regular navy skippers did. He tore out piers regularly while bringing the ship into port. He would come in with too much speed on and back down too late. The sailors used to laugh about that a lot, but he was a good skipper otherwise. I liked him a lot.

Each officer on the ship had collateral duties. I was the moral, welfare, and recreation officer. I was also the education officer for advancement of enlisted men, and there were some black enlisted men on our ship. They were all mess attendants. A couple of them were pretty bright and obviously felt frustrated about being assigned as mess attendants, so I went to the exec and told him I had a couple of mess attendants who I thought would make good boatswain's mates or coxswains in the deck division. He told me we couldn't do that because the navy had a policy of segregation, although he didn't think it was official. I then asked him if there was anything official that said we couldn't do it, and he said, "No, but I don't think we should." So I told him that unless somebody told me I couldn't do it, I was going to see that those two took the necessary courses. One of them ended up as boatswain's mate second class in the deck division, and the other one became a third class coxswain.

Nothing really negative came out of it from the white sailors. A couple of them asked me if I really thought they were qualified, and I told them the black sailors had passed all the same tests that they had taken to qualify as petty officers, so why shouldn't they be qualified? I think it was pretty well accepted, and I don't recall any repercussions. I wish now, in retrospect, I had kept in touch with them.

In January 1945, we loaded up with some cargo and troops in San Francisco and headed for Espiritu Santo in the New Hebrides. It was sort of like the movie *Mr. Roberts*, going from port to port and from tedium to apathy and back. We were just delivering supplies and dropping men off. Then, around March 1945, we got wind that we were going to be in on the Okinawa operation. We actually went to Guadalcanal for training, which was a secure base by then. Our staging base was Ulithi, which was a little spit of an island about 400 miles south of Okinawa.

Ernie Pyle, a famous World War II war correspondent. This photograph was taken aboard USS *Charles Carroll*, APA-28, off the coast of Okinawa a few weeks before he was killed.

The actual invasion came off on 1 April 1945. The code

name for the operation was Love Day. We called it April Fools' Day. On board ship we had elements of the First Marine Division, which had just come off the very rough invasion of Peleliu, and they weren't very happy about being assigned to Okinawa. The Japanese decided not to defend the beaches, but dug in about a mile back from the beaches, which was fortunate for us. Because of a coral reef, we had to transfer the troops and cargo from our LCVPs to LVTs. Because they had tracks, they could get across the coral reef, while the LCVPs couldn't. We were sitting ducks about a half a mile out from the beach, and it took about thirty minutes to complete the transfer. If the Japanese had stayed close to the beach they could have ripped us apart and I wouldn't be here telling this story today.

While we were still in Ulithi, the staging area, who should come aboard but Ernie Pyle, the famous war correspondent. We were all wondering why he was in the Pacific after spending so much of the war in Europe. Another question we had was, "Why was he coming aboard an attack transport? Why didn't he go aboard a battleship, or something like that?" Then we found out he liked to talk to the enlisted men to get stories for his articles. But he didn't like them so much that he wanted to eat with them or berth with them. He had his own room up in officers' country, and he ate in the wardroom with us. Then, much to my consternation, I found out he was going to be in my boat during the landings. I thought, "That's all I need; here I am a twenty-one-year-old ensign in charge of taking in seven boats to the beach with all these marines and cargo, and I don't need an Ernie Pyle looking over my shoulder." Fortunately, the weather was rough and nasty. In those open boats you were soaked before you were a few yards from the ship, so he decided to go up to the "Line of Transfer" in the covered gig of our boat group commander, Lieutenant Wishmeyer. Then he boarded my boat for the last few hundred yards where he would then get in an LVT for going over the reef and on to the beach. That was the last time I saw him. Seventeen days later he went over to a little island called Ie Shima, just off the coast of Okinawa, which the marines were securing, and was killed by a sniper.

We had some casualties, but that was later on. The Japanese left a few snipers close to the beach, and at night if anybody lit up a cigarette or stuck their head up they got nailed. We lost a doctor and a corpsman— members of the beach party—that way. But other than them, we didn't have any casualties.

By about the eighth day, we started really having problems with kamikazes. We were relatively protected because out on the perimeter were the destroyer escorts and destroyers, which took the brunt of most of those attacks. The other fortunate thing for us was that we had a leaking main rudder shaft, and we were taking on a lot of water. Butterfield was the skipper at the time, and he reported this to the senior officer afloat. We were then given priority for unloading our troops and cargo, so that by the eighth day, when the kamikazes started penetrating the perimeter of escort ships and attacking the main fleet, we were steaming for Saipan. We had a sister ship, *Henrico*, APA-45, that took one of the kamikazes. I had some friends on her that were killed. A Val came over and dropped its bomb that exploded in one of the boiler rooms, then crashed into the bridge, killing the captain and all the senior officers. I think the surviving senior officer was a lieutenant (jg).

We got to Saipan and the divers went down to take a look at the leaking main rudder shaft, and said there was nothing they could do, so we had to go back to Pearl Harbor. Of course, we didn't mind; we were heading for the States after having been out for all of six months.

At Pearl they said we had to go into dry dock, but theirs were full, so we were told to go to Hunter's Point in San Francisco. At Hunter's Point, they did put us up in dry dock and decided that since the ship hadn't had an overhaul for a long time they would do that, too. We were in dry dock for two or three months. It was during that time that I met my future wife, who was a navy nurse.

After we got out of dry dock it was June or July 1945. The war was almost over, and we got back into this business of carrying cargo to various islands. We had just taken some cargo and troops to the Philippines and were on the way back to the States when we got word that the atomic bomb had been dropped. Unbeknownst to us, and sadly and tragically, we were right in the area where the USS *Indianapolis* went down. We didn't know anything about it until later, but we were within thirty or forty nautical miles of her when she got torpedoed.

When we got back to Hunter's Point in August 1945, they converted us to a straight transport ship. All the boats were taken off, except for the captain's gig, and the holds were restructured to accommodate troops being brought home on operation Magic Carpet. We were taking career people and their families out to where they were being stationed in Japan, China, and places like that; and bringing back sailors and others who were

**USS *Charles Carroll*, APA-28, served as an attack transport throughout the war.**

being discharged. That was the most boring time for me, this time from September 1945 until I finally got off the ship in June 1946. We were twenty-one days out, and twenty-one days back—watch on, watch off, day after day.

I was an amphibious boat officer when I came on board, so when they took all the boats off I thought I would get thirty days' leave, then be assigned to another ship. But they had a "mustanger" on board—an enlisted man who had come up through the ranks—who was the first lieutenant, and because of him I stayed aboard *Carroll*. His name was Wishmeyer, and he was a character. He enlisted in 1937 as an apprentice seaman. I don't think he had even finished high school. When the war broke out he was a chief petty officer in charge of an oceangoing tugboat, and the day after the war started he was commissioned an ensign. A couple of months later he got a spot promotion to full lieutenant. When he made full lieutenant he was assigned to an LST that was under construction somewhere up in Minnesota. When it was finished he was supposed to sail it down the Mississippi River on its shakedown cruise, but he got this crew of greenhorns and reservists—salesmen who had gotten direct commissions—people like that. He said, "I'm not taking this damn ship with this crew aboard anywhere." He refused, and the navy caved in and assigned him to *Carroll* as the first lieutenant.

The first lieutenant is sort of like the housekeeper of the ship, and he decided he needed an assistant first lieutenant, somebody to do his paperwork. He wasn't very good at that, so unfortunately, he picked me, and that's what I did until I had enough points to go home.

# USS *LCI(L)-981*

## JOHN F. HARRINGTON

*John F. Harrington was born in 1924 in Charleston, South Carolina. He was in his third year of college in November 1942 when he received a notice from his draft board to report for his pre-induction physical. He promptly went to the local navy recruiter and signed up for the navy's officer candidate program, better known then as the V-12 program. For almost two years Harrington served in the Pacific aboard the USS LCI(L)-981, helping bring it back to the United States with a skeleton crew at the war's end, and leaving it as its last captain before it was decommissioned and scrapped. After the war Harrington returned to Chicago, Illinois, where he had met his future wife while a midshipman at Northwestern University. They married in 1948, and later moved to Los Angeles where they raised four children. Harrington, now a widower, is retired and lives in Pacific Palisades, California.*

I went on active duty 1 July 1943 and reported to the University of South Carolina, where I spent one semester. Our group was then sent to Norfolk, Virginia, where we encountered a chief petty officer who had been a wrestling coach at a major university. He delighted in walking into our barracks and looking into the one G.I. can we had. If he found a single scrap of paper in it he would kick it across the room and demand that we clean it out immediately.

December in Norfolk is very cold. The chief would take us out on the field and have us stand motionless at parade rest with our rifle butts on the ground until one of us, because of the cold, could no longer hang on to the gun. He would then make everyone run around the track with his rifle held high above his head yelling, "I am a shit bird!" We all swore that if we were commissioned and ran into that chief again we would make him stand at attention for hours.

On 15 January 1944, I reported to Northwestern University Midshipman School in the heart of Chicago. On 10 May, I was commissioned an ensign in the United States Naval Reserve, and while we were celebrating, the sadistic chief petty officer from Norfolk walked in. But he was no longer a chief. He was now a lieutenant junior grade and outranked us. We shook hands all around and he told us how proud he was that we had made it. I'm sure that he believed that by being such a son-of-a-bitch he had made men of us.

I was then sent to Orange, Texas, to report aboard the USS *LCI (L)-981* on 21 May 1944. A disinterested enlisted man on gangway watch signed me aboard while examining me as if wondering whether to keep me. I looked about at my new home, which appeared to be a lot of wrinkled sheet metal badly welded together. It was surely no battleship *Iowa*.

I joined the navy because my mother, father, aunt, and uncle all had served in the navy in World War I. There was also a large navy yard in Charleston and the fleet was often anchored in our harbor. From early childhood I had been brainwashed *Navy*! But now, looking at this LCI, I thought I had done a very foolish thing.

The executive officer, Lt. (jg) Max Mayo, came out and shook my hand warmly, and I began to feel a little better. We sat in his cabin and he explained to me that I was already well qualified to assume the duties of morale officer, commissary officer, communications officer, damage-control officer, ship's stores officer, etc. And now I understood why he had greeted me so effusively. His working life had all but ended aboard *LCI(L)-981*. He then took me to the captain, Lt. (jg) Thurman J. Bailey, who grunted and told me to be on the conn at 0600 in the morning. I was.

That next morning Captain Bailey took the ship out and tried to tear her apart. He got her up to flank speed, about seventeen knots, and I looked around for a life vest; I was sure she was going to self-destruct. But the captain moored her safely that evening and the other officers went ashore to lap up the nightlife of Orange, Texas. They left me in command of the ship, sensing I would not likely be boarded by Japanese that night.

On 8 June 1944, we sailed for the Panama Canal and went through with one other LCI and a destroyer. On the Pacific side, the swift destroyer left us, while we two LCIs plowed on for the next sixteen days toward the Society Islands. For a few days gulls followed us out to salvage the leavings of our mess trays as we dumped them over the fantail. The gulls soon left us, as one man said, "because they knew there was a war out there some place and the chow ain't worth the risk."

During that period I learned that our crew, a number of whom were over forty years of age and excellent at their jobs, had been on a training ship at Little Creek, Virginia, training crews for other LCIs. That wonderful assignment ended one day when their training ship was beached and some girls in swimsuits asked if they could come aboard. No sailor who ever lived would have said no. The ensuing party was such a blast that nobody realized the tide had gone out and the ship was stuck on the beach until the next tide. Two days later the entire crew was sent to Texas to pick up a new ship and head out to where the shooting was.

Ens. John Harrington, a 90-Day Wonder—one of many thousands of young men who became naval officers after three months of intensive training. Photograph taken in Shanghai, China, aboard USS *LCI(L)-981.*

After sixteen days at sea we at last saw the beautiful island of Bora Bora rise above the horizon. We moored dockside in a lagoon so clear you could see the coral bottom. We refueled and took on water and provisions, and that evening I was again the officer of the deck while my superiors went to the officers' club.

Early next morning, a commander strode aboard after stationing his men along the dock to make certain none of us could get ashore. He told our captain that the previous evening some of our men had stolen a washing machine from his base and he demanded to interview the crew, man by man. Not a single wide-eyed sailor knew nothing about no washing machine, so the commander searched the ship and easily found it. Again, he summoned each sailor but all remained blissfully ignorant, and some were even affronted by the implication, except for one young sailor. The commander intimidated this boy so much that he talked. The commander smiled triumphantly, and suggested to our captain that we transfer this fellow ashore so he wouldn't find himself swimming alone in the middle of the Pacific one dark night. Then he kicked our ship out of paradise.

We pushed on to places like Pago Pago, Manus, and Hollandia, and things began to get serious. We took troops aboard and headed for the Japanese-held island of Morotai. General MacArthur, who considered this operation one of the last stepping-stones on his long-promised return to the Philippines, was along in the cruiser *Nashville*. On 15 September our ship and many others could get no closer to the beach than about fifty yards, so our troops had to wade ashore in water up to their chests, with their rifles held high above their heads. But the Japanese offered little resistance because our planes had softened up the beaches thoroughly. The landing was a success and we headed back to Hollandia, New Guinea.

On 15 October 1944, we took aboard 150 troops, and joined a gigantic collection of ships that stretched as far as the eye could see in all directions, and headed for the invasion of Leyte Island in the Philippines. General MacArthur was along, riding in *Nashville* again. On the third day out, our troops, having slept two nights below decks in almost airless, darkened ship conditions, began to get grumpy. They were hot and tired, and they stunk. They wanted desperately to take a shower. One of their officers asked our skipper if anything could be done. Captain Bailey had our fire hoses hooked up and pretty soon the well deck of *LCI-981* was full of laughing, naked soldiers, playing fire hoses upon each other. Within minutes every LCI in the formation was doing the same.

On 22 October, just before dawn, we lay-to in Leyte Gulf, waiting for word to hit the beach. Some of our troops were clustered in the well deck, nervously making weak jokes, when we suddenly saw flashes just off the beach. Peering through the morning mist, we began to make out the hulks of the Seventh Fleet's ancient battle wagons, slowly cruising close to shore and letting go with their main batteries. We would see the flashes from their guns, and seconds later hear the great *whoom* as their shells exploded on the shore. Our troops were now grinning like kids, which is what they really were—kids. The landing went well, but we learned later that as our troops went deeper inland the Japanese opposition grew more fierce.

On the night of 24 October, we anchored off Dulag, Leyte, and were looking south at what appeared to be a storm gathering some fifty miles away. As we watched what seemed to be lightning flashes, we did not know that this was only the beginning of what was to be the last great naval battle in history where battleships and cruisers stood toe to toe, firing their main batteries at each other. Adm. Jesse Oldendorf was collecting five of the Seventh Fleet's ancient battle wagons and stringing them across Surigao Strait. We watched star shells lighting up the sky and innocently thought this must be one hell of a storm developing. We would not have slept that night if we had known at the time that our fates were in the hands of these old battleships: *Mississippi*, age thirty-six years, *California*, *Tennessee*, and *Maryland*, all twenty-three years old, and *West Virginia*, only twenty-one years old. Further, we did not know that Adm. "Bull" Halsey, supposedly protecting the eastern approach to our helpless transports in Leyte Gulf, had been seduced northward to chase Japanese decoys. Our being unaware of our plight illustrated well that ignorance is not only bliss, but sometimes euphoria. Oldendorf beat the Japanese that night, and because he did, I'm still here.

Our ship now settled into a routine of laying smoke screens around the larger ships to hide them from Japanese aircraft that liked to come out of the morning sun and attack them. The same routine was repeated before sunset. Only occasionally would there be an air attack during the day. But soon we began to see an incomprehensible thing—at least to occidental eyes. Japanese pilots began crashing into our ships. We argued among ourselves about whether a plane that crashed had already been hit and wanted to take somebody with him, or whether the pilot chose to crash a ship, knowing he would die. Soon it became fairly obvious that the latter was the case.

Of the twelve LCIs in our group, three were hit. One was crashed by an already stricken Japanese plane. The LCI sank in five minutes. Another was hit in the stern by a plane that had wanted to hit a bigger target, but took some fire and went for the smaller LCI instead. This ship's hull was wrinkled and split, and her captain ran her aground so she wouldn't sink, but she was out of the war. However, she was put back into another type of service. According to rumor, a group of capitalist-minded G.I.'s established a thriving bawdy house in this beached vessel. A third LCI in our group, while moored to a tanker, took fragments from a bomb meant for the tanker. Three of her people were killed, including her captain, but the ship was not badly damaged. In a period of about six weeks we saw at least thirty-five kamikazes crash ships. When attacking head-on, kamikazes presented such a narrow profile that smaller ships were rarely able to hit them with antiaircraft fire.

On 6 December 1944 we beached at Dulag, Leyte, and took aboard 250 troops of the 306th Infantry. We were greatly impressed when Gen. Bob Eichelberger came down to the beach to wish good luck to the troops boarding the LCIs. Then we joined R. Adm. A.D. Struble's Ormoc Attack Group to begin what came to be thought of as perhaps General MacArthur's most brilliant move in the Philippine campaign. We made an end run around Leyte, landing at Ormoc, thus cutting Leyte in half, separating the Japanese forces from each other and their supplies on the island.

Our convoy consisted of eight destroyer transports, twenty-seven LCIs, eleven LSMs, four LSTs, twelve destroyers, nine minesweepers, two sub chasers, and four LCI rocket ships. We passed through Surigao Strait without trouble. Destroyers *O'Brien* and *Laffey* were straddled by enemy shells without harm while maneuvering in Omoc Bay. *Laffey* would later take six kamikaze hits off Okinawa and we would eventually see her towed into Leyte with her superstructure completely missing. This was probably the worst beating any ship that survived had ever taken. But she was restored and now is in the Cooper River, Charleston, South Carolina, as a museum ship and welcomes visitors aboard.

On 7 December 1944, at 0645, the third anniversary of the bombing of Pearl Harbor, our destroyers shelled the beach at Ormoc. At 0730, twelve LCIs hit the beach, followed by fifteen more. By 0930 all LCIs had put their troops ashore and retracted from the beach with no trouble. At 0934, bogeys, or unidentified aircraft, appeared on destroyer *Lamson's* radar. For the next ten hours the ships of the Ormoc Attack Group were under almost constant air attack and suffered severe losses. Destroyers *Mahan* and *Ward* were sunk, *Liddle* and *Lamson* were damaged, and *LSM-318* was abandoned after being hit. This was the most concentrated and furious action the crew of *LCI-981* would witness during the war. We saw forty-three Japanese planes shot down in those ten hours. It was like some of those bad war movies made long after the war, where the flak was so thick you felt you could almost walk across it. But I was twenty years old, and knew I was immortal.

We had returned to Leyte Gulf by the next morning, 8 December, and were happy to be in one piece. But right away we learned that General MacArthur liked our work so much that we had to pack up immediately and head out again, this time to hit Mindoro Island one week hence.

On 13 December 1944, with troops aboard, we joined Admiral Struble's Visayan Attack Force with cruiser *Nashville*, eight destroyers, thirty LSTs, twelve LSMs, thirty-one LCIs, ten large and small minesweepers, fourteen various small craft, and twelve destroyer escorts. Admiral Berkey's Close Covering Group, consisting of two light cruisers, one heavy cruiser, and seven destroyers, also went along, as did twenty-three PT boats under Lt. Cmdr. N. Burt Davis.

We departed Leyte at 1320. At about 1500 Signalman Wilbur T. Shively and I, feeling a little smug with all the firepower surrounding *LCI-981*, were idly chatting in the conning tower and keeping station when we saw a plane come over Negros Island, drop low to the water, and head for *Nashville*. We were unconcerned. It had to be one of ours. None of our cruisers or destroyers had paid it any attention. The plane, later identified as a Val, suddenly turned right and crashed *Nashville* on her port side just abaft Admiral Struble's cabin. The ship's 5-inch and 40-mm ammunition exploded, and 133 of her crew were killed. The Japanese well knew General MacArthur's preference for riding in her, but he was not aboard that day. Destroyer *Dashiell* came alongside and took off Admiral Struble and his staff. *Nashville*, escorted by destroyer *Stanly*, returned to Leyte and our attack force pushed on to Mindoro.

When we got to Mindoro our destroyers were preparing to open fire off White Beach when a large group of Filipinos, joyously waving flags to welcome us, was discovered right in the line of fire. They had brought many of their cattle along to celebrate the return of the Americans. Admiral Berkey had his ships fire a few high bursts to warn them off, and they dispersed. Berkey then told his amphibious ships not to fire on natives or cattle, to report by name when on station, and to hurry up! We did so, and shortly were debarking our troops.

At 0812 that morning, kamikazes appeared over the beach. This seemed to be the Japanese pattern; they didn't hit us coming in, but after that they reacted furiously. The USS *Talbot*, under attack, shot down one plane, but flaming wreckage hit her deck. Minutes later, our planes knocked down another one, but three more came in low over the water through heavy fire and ran at the escort carrier *Marcus Island*. The ship's guns hit one of them, but its wing tip hit the carrier and cut off the head of one man before splashing ten yards off *Marcus Island*'s starboard bow.

Three more planes appeared. One was shot down by our combat air patrol and the other two were chased away. Moments later, three more were splashed by gunfire from our ships. At about 0945, our aircraft spotted twenty more enemy planes coming in. Ten got through and began diving on the LSTs that were approaching the line of departure. The LSTs and destroyer *Moale* knocked down some, but others attacked *LST-738*. One crashed her, setting her gasoline afire and exploding her ammunition. Another tried to crash her bridge, but *Moale* knocked it down. *LST-738* continued to burn until she was sunk by one of our destroyers. Before the day was over, another ship, *LST-472*, was also lost when a kamikaze crashed her and a bomb from the plane exploded in her well deck.

Back in Leyte Gulf, we felt a kind of emotional letdown after all the action of the last ten days. A dreadful boredom settled upon the ship's company. We played checkers, read old magazines, complained about the lack of mail from home, made smoke morning and evening, and got on each other's nerves. We were twenty-nine men who rarely got off the ship. The invasion of Lingayen Gulf on Luzon was being planned for early January 1945, and we were angry and disappointed at not being included. It wasn't that we were looking for trouble; we just wanted a break in the endless monotony.

One evening while our LCI was operating alone and heading south in Leyte Gulf, I relieved the O.D. of the 2000-to-midnight watch fifteen minutes early, as was the custom, so that if there was anything special happening he could fill me in on it. Five minutes later a PBY Black Cat patrol plane came over us at about two hundred feet and asked for our recognition code. We blinked it up to him, but the plane made a tight circle and made the same demand. We gave the same response. When this happened a third time I called the skipper to the conn. He asked what we had told the plane, then shook his head. I had given the code that would be effective at midnight rather than the code for the current day, which still had five minutes to run. The old man grunted, mumbled something about interrupting his sleep, and went below to his cabin.

On 1 January 1945, at 0906, we came alongside the heavy cruiser USS *Portland* and took aboard a liberty party. An Annapolis ensign was in charge of them, and from him I got a glimpse of the difference between life aboard a taut cruiser and a little rag-tag LCI. The ensign, smartly dressed, kept calling me sir and was startlingly deferential. Aboard *LCI-981*, nobody ever called anybody sir. The black gang called the engineering officer, Lieutenant (jg) Caprise, by his first name, Mike. I was glad I wasn't serving in *Portland*, beautiful and powerful as she was.

On 26 January 1945, at 1050, we embarked 120 troops of the 186th Paratroopers, Eleventh Airborne. They were young, loud-mouthed, and most unhappy to be travelling at nine knots for five days instead of in an airplane that could have taken them to Luzon somewhat faster. We heard a great deal about that comparison from these restless, aggressive young men who were more accustomed to practicing their dangerous trade of jumping out of planes. On 31 January at 0830, we disembarked our unhappy guests at Nasugbu, southwestern Luzon, to the relief and pleasure of us and them. We later learned that they had been in on the taking of Manila.

On 7 February, we beached at Mindoro where we met some B-24 bomber pilots who kindly invited us to fly over Borneo with them at night while they dropped bombs and empty beer bottles that sounded just like falling bombs to deprive the Japanese of a good night's sleep.

On 2 March 1945, we anchored in Puerto Princessa Bay, Palawan Island, and took a small boat ashore to see the city. We passed two Japanese floatplanes sitting in shallow water near the shore, their wings and fuselages full of holes. Walking through the town, we met a middle-aged priest sadly looking at the remains of his church, which had been destroyed by our aircraft. We came across a fenced-off area where some soldiers were digging with shovels. There was a long narrow trench in the ground with some boards covering part of it. We learned from the soldiers that when we were heading to attack Mindoro in December 1944, the Japanese on Palawan thought we were going to hit them. They herded their American prisoners of war into the trench, poured gasoline over the boards covering the trench, and set them on fire. When the Americans ran out they were machine-gunned. We saw the remains of many of these men still lying on the ground where they had fallen, leg bones sticking out of rotting boots, skeletons in tattered, weather-beaten clothing. I photographed a sign placed at the site by the U.S. Army:

> REMAINS OF AMERICAN PRISONERS OF WAR MASSACRED
> BY THE JAPANESE BURIED HERE. REINTERMENT WILL
> BE MADE UPON ESTABLISHMENT OF USAF CEMETERY.
> THIS AREA IS OFF LIMITS TO ALL PERSONNEL BY
> ORDER OF THE COMMANDING GENERAL.

On 8 April 1945 we departed Puerto Princessa Bay en route for Culion Island, which housed a leper colony that had fared badly under the Japanese occupation. Our ship was loaded with provisions for the colony. Some of our crew, however, had hidden some of these foodstuffs for their own purposes. But when we docked and saw those suffering people, our guys, with downcast eyes, brought their booty onto the deck so it could be transferred to the lepers who needed it far more than did our healthy sailors.

For the next few months our ship did little but run errands, deliver replacement troops to secured locations, visit other LCIs to sample their fare and hope to hear some new jokes or scuttlebutt. LCIs often nested while at anchor. One ship would drop her stern anchor and one or two other LCIs would ask to come alongside, so we got a cross-fertilization of ideas and complaints.

In Leyte Gulf, whenever one or two Japanese planes would come over it seemed that every gun on every ship began to shoot at them, and all that shrapnel came back down, often landing on the decks of our ships. Our planes chased enemy aircraft over the ships and sometimes encountered friendly fire. Soon our fighter aircraft were ordered not to come over the bay, even if in hot pursuit. That did not prevent one of our gunners from finding a P-38, the most recognizable warplane ever, in his sights and ready to pull the trigger before his loader stopped him.

In Leyte Gulf one afternoon Signalman Wilbur Shively and I sat in the conn and watched as the battleship *Idaho* dropped her hook near us. She then told us we were in her swinging circle. As the other officers were at the officers' club on Samar Island, I was at that moment the commanding officer of our LCI, which gave me an unwarranted sense of power. "Tell that big bastard," I said to Wilbur, "that we were here first." Wilbur gave me the look of a doting father who had suddenly discovered that his only son was stupid, and then blinked out a message. I asked, "Did you tell him?" "Hell no!" he replied. "One of us has to show some sense. I told him we were moving right now, and you better crank up this tub and haul ass before that big four-stripe bastard wants to know your name and rank." At that moment I knew that one day Wilbur would make a great parent.

On 6 August 1945, an atomic bomb was dropped on Hiroshima. Three days later another one was dropped on Nagasaki. On 14 August, we got orders to return to the States to be refitted as an LCI(R), or rocket ship, to give us the firepower of a light cruiser when firing rockets while close to the beach. Almost surely this was in anticipation of the invasion of the Japanese home islands. We immediately began celebrating the fact that we would be going back to the States. Lieutenant (jg) Caprise had brought a bottle of Haig and Haig all the way from Texas, and he, Ensign Larsen, Ensign Peterson, and I went to the unoccupied troop officers' quarters, a large and private space, and began passing that bottle around. We didn't necessarily look forward to invading Japan, but we wanted to get back to the U.S. any way possible. The scotch went quickly and was almost gone when the radioman burst in shouting, "The Japs have surrendered! The goddamn war is over!" The big ships in the bay were shooting off all kinds of fireworks, so it was true. The war was over! I reflected that we had made eight combat landings and had five battle stars. Now, thank God, it was all over.

It was almost too much good news for one day. I felt I deserved another drink, but all the scotch was gone. Only warm Blatz beer remained. I, in my inexperience, quickly downed one and the ship began to roll and pitch beneath my feet. I made my way to the port ramp and leaned over just in time to disgorge precious scotch and other things into Leyte Gulf. I knew it was against navy regulations to drink alcohol aboard a vessel of the United States Navy, and now I knew why.

Our orders to return to the States were cancelled and we headed for

Shanghai. On 10 September, we anchored in Buckner Bay, Okinawa. In a few days a storm blew in and became increasingly worse. Soon all ships were ordered to weigh anchor and maneuver independently at sea to keep from being thrown up onto the beach. We tried to haul in our anchor but couldn't because of the powerful wind, so we cut the anchor cable and headed out of the bay. Soon we were in swells as high as our conning tower—perhaps fifty feet high. Heading into the wind, we would ride to the crest and a moment later come crashing down into the trough like a fat kid on a see-saw when an even fatter kid on the other end suddenly jumps off. The little ship groaned and shuddered, and the seams in her well deck split. Seawater poured into Number One compartment, and we pumped it out continuously for about ten hours. At least a third of the crew got seasick, and I believe nine-tenths of us prayed.

When the storm subsided we anchored in the calm of Buckner Bay and went ashore just to get the feel of solid land under our feet. We saw a Liberty ship that the storm had flung onto the beach, where she lay on her side. We were able to walk completely around this unfortunate ship, grateful that our little LCI was not there with her.

On 26 September we departed Okinawa for Shanghai and arrived at the mouth of the Yangtze River on the 28th. Our flag ship, USS *St. Paul*, blinked back to us to move from astern the cruiser to a station about one hundred yards dead ahead of her because floating mines had been reported in these waters. Implicit in *St. Paul's* message was that she felt it was far better to lose a LCI than risk a cruiser. On the 29th we took aboard a river pilot, Mr. Tsu, and the next morning started up the Whangpoo River for Shanghai with Mr. Tsu calling course, speed, and rudder, while I repeated these through the voice tube down to the helmsman. We docked across from the city known as the Paris of the Orient.

In Shanghai, we met many White Russians who had been driven out of Russia during the Russian Civil War. They had made their way to Harbin or Vladivostok, and then down to Shanghai, which during the 1930s was probably the most wide open city in the world. Nobody asked questions in Shanghai. In the home of a young White Russian girl I saw a photo on her piano of a Russian officer holding the reins of his beautiful horse. He was her late father, who with his wife had fled for their lives years earlier.

Many people had been under house arrest during the Japanese occupation, but we met none with tales of significant mistreatment. The city was still wide open when we were there. *Life* magazine said there were twenty thousand prostitutes working the streets after the war. We saw countless beggars on the streets, and women sitting on the curb along the main street—Nanking Road—with dead babies in their arms, rocking them and crying their hearts out. We saw bodies floating down the Whangpoo River and young urchins with boat hooks pulling the bodies out of the water, stripping them of anything of value, then tossing them back into the river.

On 11 October 1945, at Nangpo, China, we loaded two hundred troops of the Chinese Nationalist Army and took them across the straits to Formosa. As we approached the docks at Kiirun, some fifty Corsairs came roaring over the ships at yardarm height, and then over the pier to impress upon the Japanese ashore that it might be unwise to restart the war.

I saw a captured Japanese freighter docked one hundred yards ahead of us and walked down to look it over. Marching along the dock toward me were about 150 Japanese soldiers in formation, led by one of their own. I started to sweat and looked straight ahead, but when they were about ten yards from me they all began grinning and bowing and saluting. I grinned back and saluted, holding the salute until the last row had passed.

Back in Shanghai on 3 November, Lt. (jg) Austin Hyde reported aboard to assume command of *LCI- 981*. Captain Bailey, now a full lieutenant, tossed his jg bars at me and said goodbye. Mr. Hyde called me into his cabin to tell me that Bailey said I was capable of handling the ship. I nodded. Hyde then told me that he had never been on any kind of ship before, and had been at a desk during the war in Norfolk, Virginia. "Damn," I thought, "I have to take this scow across the ocean with a captain who has no qualifications even to be aboard a ship."

A few days later, he and I were walking along a street in Shanghai when he let me know that according to navy protocol, I must walk at his left, the superior officer always being on the right. I refrained from telling him what a commander at Northwestern had told us; that rank among junior officers is like virtue among whores.

On 16 December 1945, after two wonderful months in this oriental Paris, we prepared to cast off and head for San Pedro, California. Many experienced people from the crew had gone home for discharge and we were crossing the Pacific with many billets inadequately filled. We reached

Saipan on Christmas Day 1945, and four days later were sent to Apra Harbor, Guam. We moored to the dock at Apra, and Ens. Don Larsen went ashore on ship's business. We anchored out for an hour, and then I headed the ship back to bring her alongside the USS *Hidalgo*, a transport, to pick up Larsen. We were making a normal, easy approach—one-third ahead on the port engine, right standard rudder. I asked the engine room for all engines back full speed to stop our forward motion and let our bow drift toward the larger ship—strictly routine. But the ship leaped ahead! The engine room answered, "All back full," but gave me all *ahead* full instead. I called down again and they gave the right response but the wrong direction. I yelled, "All stop! All stop!" But the ship, with her rudder over, buried her nose into *Hidalgo*'s portside, punching a hole ten feet in diameter into the innocent ship well above her waterline. Mr. Hyde, our new skipper, spent the next hour listening to the captain of *Hidalgo* ranting about, "You goddamn college boys!"

Two days later, on Saipan, En. Larsen left the ship for medical reasons and Lieutenant (jg) Scott left the ship to go home for discharge. En. Alan Borst came aboard, and he, Quartermaster Frank Boettcher, and I stood OD watches around the clock all the way home. It was rare for an enlisted man to stand officer of the deck watch in a commissioned navy ship at sea, but captains do not stand routine watches and Boettcher did a fine job.

On 24 January 1946, we entered Pearl Harbor and one glorious week later left for San Pedro. We arrived at San Pedro, California, on 10 February. It had taken us almost two months to get back to the States. On 6 March, Mr. Hyde woke me to say he had a severe ulcer and would turn himself in to the hospital. I became captain of USS *LCI-981* and took her to San Diego on 4 April for decommissioning.

On 3 May 1946, with only eight people left in the crew out of the original twenty-nine, we mustered on the quarterdeck and tore her tattered ensign down. The ship had been in commission twelve days less than two years and this was the end of her career. She was to be sold for scrap shortly thereafter. We took photos, shook hands all around, and promised to stay in touch, then went our separate ways. I was the only one of her original crew still aboard, and it was not as joyous a day as I had thought it would be.

# My Flight with
# Lt. Arthur G. Elder

## BERNARD ISAACS

*Mr. Bernard Isaacs was born in Independence, Wisconsin, in 1921, and was
one of seven children born to Jewish immigrant parents. Bernard's mother,
Hannah Bernhardt, was born in Lithuania and was the daughter of a
rabbi. His father, Max M. Isaacs, was born in Germany. Bernard was living at the YMCA in Eau Claire, Wisconsin, when the United States entered
World War II. On 8 July 1942, he enlisted in the U.S. Navy. After graduation from a special three-month program, he was made a chief petty
officer and was assigned to training black naval recruits, eventually becoming a mentor to one of the first African Americans to be commissioned in
the U.S. Navy. He then applied for and was accepted into an officers'
training program. Upon completion of his training he was assigned to an
LCI(L) and was sent to the Pacific, where he participated in landings in
the Philippines. Isaacs left the navy in 1946 as a full lieutenant. He is now
retired and lives in Lyndhurst, Ohio, with his wife, Amy.*

One of the really foolhardy things I did while in the navy happened
while our ship was anchored at the island of Mindoro, in the Philippines.
There was a naval air base nearby with a squadron of B-24s. Some of the
pilots liked to swim near our ship and enjoy a meal with us as we always
had frozen meat, jackrabbit from Australia and lamb from New Zealand.
I was enamored with some of their stories of long-distance flights to the
coast of French Indochina to spot Japanese shipping.

As we were temporarily inactive I thought it would be a nice idea

**Ens. Bernard Isaacs, son of European Jewish emigrants. He was a mentor to one of the first of thirteen African Americans to be commissioned as U.S. naval officers, then went on to become commissioned himself. Photograph taken aboard USS *LCI(L)-965*.**

to see another part of the world—to go on one of their missions. The date was 19 February 1945. The flyers sent a jeep over early in the morning to pick me up that day. They had assigned me to fly with a swashbuckling pilot by the name of Lt. Arthur C. Elder, from Dallas, Texas, who had a cocker spaniel at his side when he flew. I didn't know who he was at the time, but found out later he was the navy's top ace for sinking enemy tonnage in the Pacific theatre, and he was in a long-term contest with Commander Norman "Bus" Miller. Some pilots later told me that Elder was one of the few pilots who routinely carried four 500-pound bombs on his flights, which were characterized as scouting missions.

We flew for approximately five hours before reaching the coast of French Indochina, where we spotted three ships heading up the coast. One of the ships was armed, one was a supply ship, and one carried fuel. Lieutenant Elder flew inland and then came out almost directly in line with the three ships. I was standing behind a metal plate behind the pilot when the nose, waist, and tail gunners started firing on the ships. I looked down at the cocker spaniel next to Lieutenant Elder and saw him put both paws over his ears.

It was then that I felt I was in a situation I really hadn't bargained for. The pilot dropped two bombs that fell short of the ships from five hundred feet over the water. The sky was black with flack. I thought, "How can they miss us?" as we circled for another run at them, dropping the other two bombs, again missing the ships. All I could think of at that moment was, "Nobody knows where I am." The captain of my ship was unaware that I was on this mission. Then there was my poor mother with my brother a POW in Germany.... All of these things were going through my mind as we circled around for another run of strafing at five hundred feet over the water. Again we escaped and headed south over non-hostile water, then inland over villages.

Bernard Isaacs and his wife Amy Ruth Isaacs. Photograph taken in 1999.

We returned approximately forty-five minutes later for another strafing run on the same Japanese ships—again from only five hundred feet. We then headed back to base. I was emotionally drained and thankful to be heading back to Mindoro—alive. On the return flight I had a chance to talk with the crew and, to a man, they expressed unhappiness over their plight as being the only crew in the squadron carrying bombs and taking these extremely high risk, low altitude missions. In retrospect, amphibious landings were a piece of cake.

When we arrived back at Mindoro the plane was inspected for damage and it was found that the fuel tanks were almost empty. Maybe the other flyers were playing a trick on me by giving me what they thought was the ultimate thrill. The conclusion to that flight was that our submarines were notified, and they reportedly sank all three Japanese ships the next day.

> "Bringing those young boys aboard ship, those gung-ho young men who thought they were going to whip the Japs single-handed; seeing them with burns, gun shot wounds, shrapnel wounds—seeing them with their ribs sticking out—it was sad."

# The Mustanger

## LT. CMDR. WARREN DECIOUS, USN (RET.)

*Lt. Cmdr. Decious was born in 1908 in Lassen County, California. He enlisted in the U.S. Navy in 1928 on his nineteenth birthday and served on a variety of ships and at different shore stations during the interwar years. He was married and had two sons by the time the United States entered World War II, and during the war he spent most of his time serving aboard the hospital ship USS* Refuge, *AH-11. By war's end he was an ensign and retired from the navy in 1959 as a lieutenant commander in the Medical Service Corps. He now lives in Fairfield, California, and is a great-grandfather.*

*The USS* Refuge, *AH-11 was originally built and commissioned as a civilian liner, SS* President Madison. *In 1942, it was purchased by the navy and commissioned as a transport, USS* Kenmore, *AP-62. In 1944 it was converted to a hospital ship and remained as such until war's end. It was decommissioned in 1946 and scrapped in 1948.*

I am ninety-two years old and my memory is pretty fair. Christ, I'm so old some people think I helped build the pyramids. I spent half of my time in the navy as an enlisted man, and half my time as a commissioned officer. I enlisted in the navy on 3 December 1928. I was nineteen and could see that there was no work available as a civilian. There was no advertising for the military in those days, so let's just say I was accepted into the navy. They weren't recruiting because there were no appropriations to fund a navy in those days.

I had quite a career in the navy, but I never tried to make myself prominent. I knew that an enlisted man went into the navy to work and had to behave himself if he wanted to advance, and I wanted to advance. But I didn't advance very fast in those days until we started preparing for war. Then I made advancement rapidly. That was around 1938.

Early on, I was selected to go to Hospital Corps School in San Diego, California, and graduated from the four-months-long course in June 1929. I had acquired a reputation as a hard worker and got to work in the operating room, which I thoroughly enjoyed. Eventually, I got into administration.

I probably spent half of my navy career on ships, and half of it on shore. I established quite a record for sea duty as a pharmacist's mate. See, most men preferred shore duty and I made it possible for many of them to do just that. I liked sea duty. Those line officers, especially the academy graduates, were damn good personnel people. They knew how to discipline people. The medical officers, on the other hand, were commanding officers of their hospitals. They were more of the fatherly type. They were the sort who felt everybody should be forgiven at least once. That was my interpretation of them. Anyway, they were good people, and damn good doctors, especially the ones I worked with in the operating room.

Prior to the war, I did about two years of duty on the island of Guam—part of 1935, 1936, and 1937. I was in Agat and got to see the inland part of Guam and some of the beauty that a lot of people didn't get to see. The Chamorros were outstanding—the finest and most honest people I have ever lived with. I never took advantage of them, and they were most considerate of me. I delivered native babies, saved a couple of lives, and did some first aid work for shark bites on one of them.

There was a place on Guam called Shinohara's. We used to go down there and eat. Shinohara was a good man—a good businessman. One time this first class petty officer, Ralph Mettnet, asked old Shinohara, "We ever going to have war with Japan?" Shinohara was a very intelligent man and answered the question this way, "Let's say you have a nice pet dog in the backyard, and every day you go out there and beat that dog. He will back up, but some day you will back him into a corner and he will bite you." Now, the word "sanctions" wasn't used in those days, but I learned that day that sanctions don't work, because that is what we did to Japan when we cut off their supply of metals, oil, and rubber. What did they do? They went right down to the East Indies and took it, and they built a hell of a war machine to do it with.

When I was on Guam storm clouds were gathering in Europe, and the ordinary enlisted man knew that if we were having trouble with the Germans in Europe, then we were going to have trouble with the Japs. We called them "Japs" even then, and we were encouraged to call them "Japs" during the war. Now, I have to be very careful to call them "Japanese" whenever I'm around select company. But sometimes around intellectuals I still call them "Japs."

On Guam before the war there were Japanese situated in strategic places around the island. There was one we named "Okinawa." He was in Agat. By that time I had acquired four or five fighting cocks, and in the evening when the weather was nice we would get together and train these cocks. One time I said something to Okinawa, and a Chamorro friend of mine, Joaquin Carbullido, said, "He doesn't understand you." I said, "Joaquin, the hell he doesn't. That goddamn Jap understands every word we say. He probably speaks English better than either one of us." But anyway, when the Japs did invade Guam all of these Japs living there appeared in their Japanese military uniforms.

When the Japs bombed Pearl Harbor, I had just been transferred off the transport USS *Chaumont* to the naval base at Norfolk, Virginia, for reassignment. I was a first class petty officer by then and was assigned to the headquarters of the Sixth Naval District. The navy was full of older commissioned officers in those days before the war. They couldn't do a goddamn thing and didn't intend to. After the war started the navy got rid of most of them and replaced them with younger officers.

I wasn't a prisoner of war, but I had several friends who were and they didn't live long after the war. In fact, we put the entire population of one prison camp in the Philippines on our hospital ship and brought them back to the United States. And when those fellows told me about the treatment they were given by the Japs, I have never since had any sympathy for abusive people, no matter who they are.

I also knew several navy corpsmen who were on Guam when the Japs invaded and they were made prisoners of war. I saw some of them after the war was over. One of them, by the name of Johnnie Polk, married a native girl and he lived there with her and their children after the war was over. I returned to Guam some years later when I was serving on the aircraft carrier USS *Valley Forge*, CV-45. I looked him up and said,

"Well, Johnnie, how did you like your vacation in Japan?" He said, "My God, they took us from here over to the Philippines, then finally up to Japan, and they put me to work in the coal mines. We had damn few clothes, and we were barefoot. The soles of my feet were black for two years after that. They got their money's worth out of us POWs." Anyway, he didn't live so very long, either.

I remember one fellow; he was a chief petty officer and he had been a prisoner of war in the Philippines. At his camp, he was in charge of the burial pool. He told me he didn't know how he made it. He had four men to help him dig graves, and the Japs didn't feed them very much, so he went to one of the guards and told him that his men couldn't work any longer—they were just giving out. That guard went out there and whipped the hell out of them. "Now," the guard said, "they can do it." That was the sort of treatment they received. I asked the chief if he knew what happened to that guard who ordered the beatings. He said, "Yes! He was on watch in one of the guard towers when our Army Rangers came in and liberated the camp. One of them fired into that guard tower and blew that Jap all to hell."

Those Japs thought they were going to win the war, and I did too at first. I thought we were heading down the drain. However, I think the big mistake the Japs made when they hit Pearl Harbor was they didn't bring an invasion force with them. They could have taken the place; there wouldn't have been anything to it.

When the war started we sure had a lot of "4-F'ers." There were more people who were going to be priests and preachers than I ever saw before the war started. I'm talking about men who were already in the navy.

I advanced rapidly after the war started and was eventually appointed a warrant officer. That was about 1942. I was then sent to a naval hospital in Portsmouth, Virginia. Christ, there were so many people working there they didn't know if they were staff or visitors. Finally, I wrote to this lieutenant I knew down in Washington and requested sea duty. He got back to me and I was given orders to go to Baltimore and report to the USS *Refuge*, AH-11. Oh, it was good duty. Everybody had a job to do and they knew what they were supposed to do. They were a wonderful group of people. The chief nurse had been a young nurse on the USS *Relief*, AH-1, back when I was a young pharmacist's mate, and I worked with her sister in the operating room. They had navy nurses on hospital ships the whole time I was in the navy, and in those days they weren't commissioned, but they were shortly after the war started.

We were in just about every theater of war. We went to the Mediterranean and the North Atlantic. They were going to use us in the invasion of France—the Normandy landings in June 1944—but the seas were so rough that they didn't send us. There was no way we could have brought patients aboard in that weather. So we were sent into the Mediterranean and were with that group that invaded southern France. We loaded patients and took them to Naples, and from there we went to the Pacific. We went to the Philip-

Lt. Cmdr. Warren Decious, a "mustanger," one of the many enlisted men who rose through the ranks to be commissioned during the war. Photograph taken at his retirement party at Mare Island, California, in 1959.

pines, Okinawa, and the Admiralties. We would bring patients back from the combat areas to base hospitals. We would load them on board right from the beaches.

That is where I lost my desire for any more war. Bringing those young boys aboard ship, those gung-ho young men who thought they were going to whip the Japs single-handed; seeing them with burns, gun shot wounds, shrapnel wounds—seeing them with their ribs sticking out—it was sad. Those poor young men never had a chance at life. I learned to put on a veneer—to show very little emotion—but I can tell you I don't want any more of those experiences like I had during the war.

But that war did one good thing. It brought advances in surgery, prosthetic surgery, and dental surgery we never would have had if it hadn't been for that war. Later, after the war, I was given shore duty at San Diego and was attached to the Hospital Corps School that was part of the Naval Hospital there. I saw more war casualties there. They had new lips made, eyebrows, and ears. The dental people were making new jaws from grafted bone. For lips, their forearms were fixed to their mouths and tissue was grafted directly to where their new lips would be. None of this was done before the war.

While the war was still going on I had two young sons at home and I started thinking that if the war lasted long enough it wouldn't be too long before they would be of draft age. They were in what you would call middle school at that time. I thought that would really be something to be in the war and have my sons in it too. There have been wars ever since Christ was an apprentice seaman, and there are always going to be.

"Those of us who served on *Ringness* are considered
members of the *Indianapolis* Survivors Association,
and we attend their reunions every year."

# The Rescuers

## CAPT. WILLIAM C. MEYER, USN (RET.)

*Capt. William C. Meyer was born in 1913, in Ukiah, California. During
World War II, he commanded three different ships and went from ensign
to commander in five years. After World War II, he transferred from the
reserves to the regular navy. His last sea command was that of Commander Amphibious Squadron Seven in 1962, during the Cuban Missile Cri-
sis. He retired from the navy in 1968 and now lives in Oakland, California.
Captain Meyer was a "plank owner" on the first three ships he skippered.
PC-476 was one of several new types of ships introduced into the navy during World War II. Originally intended as a small patrol craft for antisubmarine defense, like other types of ships it served in a variety of roles during
the war. PC-476, along with PC-477 and PC-479, was the first PC to
transit the Panama Canal and serve in Hawaiian waters. The USS Newman, DE-205, another new class of ship introduced into the navy during
World War II, was commissioned in 1943, again with Captain Meyer as
its first skipper. The Newman remained in service throughout the war and
continued to serve in the Atlantic Reserve Fleet until 1964. It was sold as
scrap in 1966. USS Ringness was originally laid down as a destroyer escort
but was reclassified as a fast attack transport (APD) by the time it was
commissioned in July 1944. Again, Captain Meyer was the commission-
ing skipper. Ringness served in various capacities throughout the rest of
the war in the Pacific, but its most memorable role was that of rescuing
survivors of the ill-fated Indianapolis, sunk by a Japanese submarine after
having delivered parts to the first atomic bomb dropped on Japan to the
island of Tinian in the Mariana Islands.*

I was born in Ukiah, California, where my father was in charge of one of five coastal geodetic and survey observatories. Later on he became a professor of astronomy at the University of California at Berkeley. I was schooled in the Oakland/Berkeley area and entered the University of California in 1930. In the meantime, I had met then Cmdr. Chester W. Nimitz, who was the professor of naval science and commanding officer of the naval ROTC unit at Berkeley. I became acquainted with Admiral Nimitz because I went to school with his son, Chester, Jr. My dad was associated with Admiral Nimitz at the university where he assisted the NROTC staff with teaching navigation. This is also when I became interested in the navy ROTC program. So in 1930, when I entered the university, I also applied for the NROTC program and was accepted.

College professors didn't make much in those days, and my father was already putting my sister through college, so I left the university after two years and spent the next two years as a cadet seaman and finally as a quartermaster on the SS *Monterey* with the Matson Navigation Company. We sailed from San Francisco to Australia—thirteen round trips in two years. I was able to save enough money to go back to college in 1934 and graduated in 1937. In the meantime, I had gotten my commission through the NROTC in 1936, as an ensign in the Naval Reserve.

In 1937, after I graduated from college, I went to work for the Southern California Edison Company as a junior engineer, although I had no engineering experience. At the same time, I was a member of an active reserve division in Los Angeles. In 1939, all of the reserve divisions were put on alert for mobilization. We were on alert but continued with our civilian jobs until late 1940, when we received orders to report to the USS *Aldebaran*, AF-10, which was a supply ship. The captain of this ship— and I will never forget his name—was Capt. Royal W. Abbott. He was a by-the-book man. He was good, but strict. On the bridge he had a rearview mirror so he could watch what was going on behind him. He watched us every minute when we had the watch. He was an academy man and he did not trust us reservists. I don't think he ever came to trust us in the year that I was aboard.

Anyway, this ship was carrying supplies between the West Coast and Hawaii to supply the fleet. In the late summer of 1941, we had a mission of carrying cement, 6-inch coastal defense guns, ammunition, and everything else necessary to fortify the naval station at Pago Pago in American

Samoa. We were running with darkened ship because there was a rumor that a German raider was loose in the area even though we weren't at war yet.

Coming back from Samoa, between Samoa and Hawaii, smoke appeared on the horizon. An American destroyer came over to check us out. He had picked us up on his radar. We learned that he was part of a convoy of British ships being escorted by U.S. destroyers to Australia. This was before December 1941.

On 1 December 1941, we left Pearl Harbor for San Francisco, our normal routine. We got into San Francisco on 6 December, and of course on 7 December the Japanese bombed Pearl Harbor. We were all back aboard ship that Sunday afternoon, and instead of loading beans and potatoes, we loaded ammunition and made one run as an ammunition ship in mid–December.

I can't remember the exact date, but I think it was close to Christmas when we pulled into Pearl Harbor. What a mess! In the meantime, I had heard of a new class of ship being built by the navy, a PC—patrol craft. I wrote a personal note directly to Admiral Nimitz about these new ships and asked if there was a chance of getting assigned to one of them. By the end of December 1941, orders came for me to immediately proceed to New Orleans. There I found the USS *PC-476*, my first command. It was 173 feet long and designed for ASW—antisubmarine warfare. We had depth charges, sonar, and a 3-inch gun, but no radar.

We had three officers on board, myself and two ensigns. I was a lieutenant (jg) by that time. I had two "Ninety-Day Wonders," Ens. R.D. Butler and Ens. D.P. Wilber. These two ensigns were right out of the "Ninety-Day Wonder" school at Northwestern University and had never been aboard ship. I was the only one who had any sea experience.

We had forty-four enlisted men. About half were reserves, and the rest were regular navy who had come to us from other ships. My chief engineer was a machinist's mate first class by the name of J.G. Rivers—a good steam engineer. He had never seen a diesel engine, and here we had two General Motors diesel engines on the PC. That was the early part of the war, and we couldn't send people back to school for more training. Rivers learned how to maintain those diesels by reading books and on-the-job training.

When I look back, it amazes me how fast those young Americans could adjust and learn. Like these two young ensigns—you wouldn't believe how quickly they assimilated and learned the responsibilities of executive officer, engineering officer, and communications.

Right away I recognized that we needed a fourth officer. It was difficult, both physically and mentally, for me to be commanding officer and navigator and stand watches. So I wrote a formal letter to the chief of naval personnel saying we desperately needed a fourth officer so I could be relieved of navigation. By the time we got out to Hawaii we had that fourth officer, Ens. W.G. Anderson.

In April or May 1942, we were assigned to escort the USS *Long Island*, CVE-1, through the Panama Canal to the West Coast and out to Hawaii. Along with us came *PC-477* and an old World War I four-stack destroyer. We were then stationed in Hawaii for a few months until we were ordered to the South Pacific in September. There were three of us by then, *PC-476, 477,* and the *479*.

We went to Palmyra Island, then to American Samoa for refueling stops, and then to New Caledonia. Then sometime in October *PC-476* was ordered to Guadalcanal. Our assignment, once there, was to operate primarily at night in the unloading area off Lunga Roads, searching for enemy submarines. Troop and supply ships would withdraw at night because of the "Tokyo Express" coming down "The Slot." But us little boys would stay to keep the landing areas free of subs.

We were based over at Tulagi on Florida Island. On 11 October 1942, one of the battles off Cape Esperance occurred. The PT boats that were also based at Tulagi engaged the Tokyo Express that night between Cape Esperance and Savo Island and sank the Japanese destroyer *Teruzuki*, which had R. Adm. Raizo Tanaka, the squadron commander, on board.

During the conflict, one of our PT boats got completely disoriented and ended up on the other side of Cape Esperance, where it went aground behind enemy lines. *PC-476* was ordered out to see if we could rescue the boat and her crew. When we got over there, the PT boat was aground, but quite some distance offshore. We managed to tie our mooring lines to the stern of the boat and pull it off. The forward part of the boat was damaged and taking some water, so we gave the crew some pumps, and they took off on their own back to Tulagi.

On our way over to rescue the PT boat, we saw a ship's boat dead in the water. It was left over from the night's engagement. En route back to Tulagi we found the boat again and towed it back to base. In that boat was a large suitcase with an admiral's uniform, plus his sword and dagger. This was Admiral Tanaka's "abandon ship" kit, as we called it. According to the reports I have been able to find, he was rescued and went ashore on Guadalcanal that night. I learned all of this years later. At the time, we didn't know who he was.

Also on that boat was a roll of maps in Japanese, showing our gun positions on Guadalcanal. When we got back to Tulagi that night I got one of the PT boats to take me, with all of this stuff that was in that boat, over to Guadalcanal where the headquarters for Marine Intelligence was based.

On 3 January 1943, we received orders to proceed to a point off Santa Isabel Island in the Solomons to rendezvous with the USS *Nautilus* to assist in removing some people who were getting off Bougainville Island: nuns, plantation owners, and some children. Santa Isabel

Capt. William C. Meyer, a graduate of the NROTC program at U.C. Berkeley. During World War II he commanded three different ships and was involved in the rescue of survivors of USS *Indianapolis*. Photograph taken shortly before his retirement in 1968.

is north of Guadalcanal. *Nautilus* had gone in and picked them up off the beach on Bougainville with the help of some Australian coast watchers.

Here we were with darkened ship and no radar, but with our god-given eyes and good navigation, we rendezvoused with *Nautilus* and took aboard—I think it was twenty-two people—Americans and Australians. The nuns were from the Long Beach area of California. We brought them back to Guadalcanal and put them aboard one of our troop transports for transportation to New Zealand. That was our second rescue mission.

By January-February of 1943, the situation on Guadalcanal was pretty well secured, and in June 1943, I was relieved of command and brought back to the States. I was sent to Charleston Naval Shipyard and became commanding officer of the USS *Newman*, DE-205—a new destroyer escort. We operated in the Atlantic and Mediterranean doing convoy duty in late 1943 and early 1944. I turned command of *Newman* over to my executive officer, Robert Thieme, on 1 July 1944, in New York, where I took command of the USS *Ringness*, APD-100, named after a Dr. Ringness, who was killed on Guadalcanal. It was a high-speed destroyer transport. We carried four landing craft and could carry up to 150 troops.

We went out to Guadalcanal and joined Task Force Baker, which was to be the eastern landing force on Okinawa. This was now getting into 1945. We had 5-inch guns, hedgehogs, depth charges, and sonar, so they used us an escort for other ships. We were involved in escorting ships from Saipan and Guam to Okinawa, and on one of those trips we were escorting a group of LSTs. I was standing up on the bow with one of the sailors and chatting, which was one of my habits. It was a wonderful day; we had calm seas and were steaming along, zigzagging in our patrol area, when the general alarm sounded. I looked up and there was a periscope, and a torpedo was coming towards us on our portside. The submarine was between us and the convoy. There was another torpedo that went astern of us, and I was almost paralyzed. I started up the ladder to the bridge, and that torpedo went right underneath us. Now, was it a torpedo or wasn't it? I later read in a Naval Institute paper that this was a submarine with *kaitens* aboard, which were manned suicide torpedoes. Anyway, we didn't pick them up on sonar, but we went in and laid a big depth charge pattern and there was a terrific explosion! The water went 100–150 feet into the air with debris. I think it had to be one of those *kaitens*, and I picked up some of the debris to prove it.

We also had radar picket duty off Okinawa. Those who had picket duty on Station Fifteen, up in the northwest corner, were lined up with the route that the kamikazes took from Kyushu down to Okinawa. *Hugh P. Hadley* and *Evans*, both destroyers, were almost beaten to death by kamikazes one day, and we were ordered up to assist them because we had a medical team aboard. Plus, we had the space to take survivors on board. Those ships were all beat up, but we got the survivors back to Kerama Retto, where we had a hospital ship.

We were on picket duty to the west of Okinawa one night when we came under attack. We had a kamikaze coming directly at us. It was 0200 and we were at general quarters, but we didn't fire at the plane because

I knew that the flashes from the guns would give him a definite target. We went to flank speed and I ordered hard-left rudder when the plane was about five miles out, according to our radar. I'm not exaggerating when I say you could have reached up and touched the wheels of that plane as it flew over our stern and crashed into the water. When we have our ship reunions, some of the men still come up to me and say, "Captain, you saved our lives."

After Okinawa, we went to the Philippines, to train for the invasion of Kyushu Island, which was supposed to start on 15 November 1945. Our job was to carry in UDT—underwater demolition teams. During this training period, we were pulled from training to escort two jeep carriers to Ulithi Atoll. This was late in July 1945. After we got them to Ulithi, we were ordered to return to the Philippines as fast as possible in order to continue with our training exercises. About halfway back we received a message telling us to proceed at our best speed to a point somewhere between where we were and Guam. This was on 2 August 1945. The message read, "SURVIVORS IN THE WATER. PROCEED AT BEST SPEED TO EFFECT RESCUE."

We cranked up to twenty-one knots and arrived on the scene on 3 August and started picking up survivors. The first group we picked up were from three rafts tied together. I saw a man standing up in khakis, waving his arms. And who was it but Capt. Charles B. McVay III, commanding officer of the USS *Indianapolis*. I think there were nine enlisted men with the captain in that group, and we continued to pick up men from 9:00 in the morning until about 1:00 that afternoon. We picked up a total of thirty-nine, including Captain McVay. The USS *Register*, another APD, covered another area, and over the horizon were other ships in the rescue mission. It was amazing how spread out the survivors had become. They were all traumatized, understandably, and some of them had serious sunburns. Captain McVay was quiet, but I could see that he was disturbed. I sat there with him and we talked about what the ship was doing when they were torpedoed. At first he didn't want to include in his report the fact that they weren't zigzagging, but he came around to the fact that the sinking would be investigated and all the facts would come out eventually, and it would be best if he laid it all out in his report.

Captain McVay was later court-martialed for not zigzagging his ship and thus causing the loss of his ship. He was the only navy captain in the history of the United States Navy ever to be court-martialed for losing his ship in combat. He was court-martialed for political reasons; somebody had to be a scapegoat. This is my opinion, but it was the port director on Guam who should have been court-martialed for sending a capital ship through waters that he knew had enemy submarine activity. The USS *Underhill*, a destroyer escort, had been lost in the same area to a submarine just two weeks before. *Indianapolis* should never have been sent alone. Captain McVay had requested an escort, but was told there were none available. That, I cannot believe. They could have ordered us over from Ulithi to be an escort. Unfortunately, in 1968 or 1969, Captain McVay committed suicide, and only recently did the president of the United States and Congress exonerate him.

Those of us who served on *Ringness* are considered members of the *Indianapolis* Survivors Association, and we attend their reunions every year. They think we're angels because they were in the water for four days, and to have been able to survive for that time under those conditions— no water, no food, under the sun, and the sharks—it's amazing!

The sailors on *Ringness* and our medical team did a wonderful job of getting the survivors cleaned up and to sickbay. They donated clothes to these men, sometimes right off their backs.

I didn't see Admiral Nimitz during the war, but after the war, when I was a professor of naval science in the NROTC program at Berkeley, he had retired from the navy and was living at his home in Berkeley. He would call me and say, "Meyer, bring a couple of midshipmen up here. I want to play some horseshoes." He loved to play horseshoes, so I would go up to his house with a couple of midshipmen, and Mrs. Nimitz would bake fresh bread. After the horseshoe game we would sit there in their living room, eat fresh bread, and just chat. That was the kind of man he was.

My wife and I go to four or five ship reunions every year. That's what I really love, getting together with these men who were kids then, having a few beers, and telling sea stories. Last year was the first year we didn't go, and that was because of health reasons. I'm eighty-seven now.

"I was just standing there, looking around, when I realized
that those sounds whizzing past my head were bullets."

# Japanese-Language Officer

## WILLARD H. ELSBREE

*Mr. Elsbree was born in 1920 in Preston Hollow in upstate New York.
After graduation from high school he went to Dartmouth College for two
years before transferring to Harvard University. He graduated from Harvard in June 1941, and in the fall of 1942, volunteered to go to Boulder,
Colorado, to the navy's Japanese-language school. He served as a Japanese-
language officer in Hawaii, then with the Fifth Marine Division on Iwo
Jima. After the war was over, he was sent to Japan as part of the occupation, where he remained until his return to the United States and his discharge from the navy. He then went back to Harvard, where he earned a
Ph.D. Elsbree is a retired university professor and lives in Athens, Ohio.*

*At the time of the Japanese attack on Pearl Harbor in December 1941,
the U.S. Navy had only about a dozen officers who were fluent in the Japanese language. The first stateside Japanese-language school was in Berkeley, California. However, because of the evacuation of Americans of
Japanese ancestry from the West Coast, it was moved to Boulder, Colorado.
By war's end, the school had produced more than 1,000 graduates at various levels of proficiency.*

In the fall of 1942, I was in Cambridge, Massachusetts, visiting a friend
who said, "There is a navy recruiter in town, recruiting for the navy's
Japanese-language school. I'm going by to interview; why don't you come
along?" That is how I first encountered Lt. Cmdr. Hindmarsh. After a
brief conversation, he said, "Do you want to be in Boulder the first,
fifteenth, or thirtieth of December?" I gulped and said, "I guess the first
of December."

171

I think this was at a stage in the war when the navy wanted to vastly expand its Japanese-language program, and Hindmarsh was going around the country, recruiting people wherever he could find them. Too, I think the navy realized they weren't going to find too many people who had much experience in Japanese, so they were looking for people whose background made them suitable candidates. Perhaps he was also influenced by the fact that he had been at Harvard and had known my brother who preceded me at Harvard, and who had been there at the same time as Lt. Cmdr. Hindmarsh.

The understanding was that I would go in as a "naval agent." I'm not quite sure what the exact definition of a naval agent is, but presumably it was somebody whose services the navy wanted to contract for without having them enlist right then.

I was then instructed to go home and wait for further instructions. The instructions I eventually received indicated a change in plans. I was to report to the nearest naval recruiting station for induction as a yeoman—a yeoman second class, as I remember. It took a couple of trips to the naval recruiting station before everything was straightened out.

I was sworn in and then sent to Samson Naval Base, which was on Lake Seneca in New York State, for outfitting. I was then put on a train and arrived in Boulder, Colorado, around the first of December 1942. My stay in Boulder was an interesting one. I look back at it with many fond memories and realize what an unusual conglomeration of people constituted the language school. Some of the instructors were Nisei. I remember a Miss Kishimoto—a tall, very good-looking lady. One of the more striking figures was a Mr. Katsura, who was a rather aristocratic-looking type.

There were a number of Caucasian instructors, too. I remember a Mr. Ross, who had been a missionary in Japan. He was one of my first instructors and a helpful introducer to the language. A Mrs. Florence Walne was the director of the school.

After I had been there for a few months, it turned out that it was all a mistake; we shouldn't have been outfitted in uniforms as yeomen. We should have been made naval agents. This involved sending back home for our civilian clothes and turning in our uniforms. We did not get back into uniform until we were commissioned, toward the end of our stay at Boulder.

After my graduation from Boulder in early 1944, I was sent to Pearl

Harbor, where I was assigned to JICPOA—Joint Intelligence Center Pacific Ocean Areas—in the translation section. The translation section was divided up into small units, called "hans," each specializing in particular types of Japanese documents. I was assigned to the weather section, translating documents and weather maps. I would say more of it was of historical interest than immediate interest. I think the most significant item I remember working on was a codebook, which had been captured on Guam or Saipan. This book made it possible to translate the Japanese weather code, which was highly useful.

A Commander Steele was in charge of the translation section. He was a slight, very crusty and profane character. It was my understanding that he had been in the regular navy, but had to drop out before the war for physical reasons, but came back at the outbreak of war.

While I was at Pearl Harbor, I was assigned to the Fifth Marine Division for the invasion of Iwo Jima. I have no idea why I was selected, and the only special training I received was an hour or two on a pistol range. I turned out to be a very poor shot, and as far as I know I never even hit the target.

I was assigned to the headquarters unit, presumably as an interpreter. I was slated to go ashore on D+2, but I'm sure it was the following day or even the day after that before the situation was secure enough to allow a noncombatant like myself to be sent in. Meanwhile, the ship I was on was being used as a temporary hospital ship. The wounded were brought aboard in cargo nets. And from the ship, we could see the fighting going on. It was strange; I was aware of all the gunfire, but it seemed oddly distant to me. When I did go ashore, I have to admit to a sort of dazed feeling. Everything seemed completely confused. There didn't appear to be any line of action or order. I remember seeing men running towards me, and then throwing themselves down on the ground, and a big shell exploding right behind them. I was just standing there, looking around, when I realized that those sounds whizzing past my head were bullets. I finally had the sense to throw myself down on the ground. I became aware that there were dead and wounded men all around me, as well as dismembered bodies.

After the first day, I dug a foxhole near the edge of the airfield. I shared it with Commander Erskine, who was the chief language officer of the division. At one point we were concerned with the shrapnel from shells being fired from our own ships.

On Iwo Jima there wasn't a lot of interpreting to do. I remember just one Japanese prisoner who was brought into the headquarters unit. He was absolutely petrified with all of the language people gathered around him, plying him with cigarettes, food, and whatnot. But he didn't have much information to offer.

The other major work we did was sorting over documents, which had been captured, deciding which ones should be sent back to Pearl Harbor for further work and which ones could be disposed of locally. I don't remember coming across any particularly valuable documents.

Willard H. Elsbree, Japanese-language officer (right). Photograph taken with friend John Congleton in Honolulu, 1944.

At the end of the Iwo Jima operation, I went back to Pearl, where I stayed until the end of the war. In fact, the whole translation section was packed up and flown out to Guam, at which point we were dispersed to various units. I ended up with the Fourth Marine Regiment, which was one of the first units to land in post-surrender Japan. There was, of course, a good deal of apprehension on our part, as well as by the Japanese. My apprehension had nothing to do with physical safety, but with my ability to deal with the language. It was a well-founded apprehension, since I found out from having dealt with weather terminology for over a year, it was poor preparation for the myriad activities that I was called upon to interpret after I got ashore. One of the very first jobs I had involved going over the electrical wiring on one of the buildings in Yokosuka with one of the electricians. I was dealing with language I didn't even understand in English, let alone in Japanese.

I never had any physical fear any time I was in Japan. Even when traveling alone, I never felt threatened in any way, shape, or manner. In fact, there were almost no instances of attacks on American forces. I don't remember any being reported in the Yokosuka area.

I might add that I was not the only interpreter attached to the outfit. There were two other Boulder boys, Jim Durbin and Sam Brock. Then there were at least three local Japanese interpreters.

The first morning we were there in Yokosuka, we took a walk through the town with the marines—a show of force, I guess. There was almost no one on the streets. The few people who were out were almost all men, and none of them would look directly at us. But if you looked out the corner of your eye, you saw people peeking out from behind curtains. And it was the children who led to the breaking down of the barriers between the Japanese and the American servicemen. The soldiers tossed the children candy whenever they saw any, and the barriers came down fast after that.

The work was rather interesting and involved many things, including learning the role of the Japanese police, and much of my work involved working with the Yokosuka Police Department. For example, if you wanted to get anything done, you went to the police instead of city hall. Whenever there was a black market or any kind of criminal case, the Japanese police always went to the Korean community to look for suspects. The more one observed this sort of thing, the more aware one became of the similarities between the status of the Koreans in Japan and the status of African Americans in the United States.

A lot of my work involved translating in incidents where sailors were brought in after having drunk too much while on liberty and beating up on Japanese. They were brought in by the marine MPs, and I must say the marines took great delight in bringing them in.

A minor assignment we Boulder boys occasionally drew, or divided up among ourselves, involved high-ranking officers, usually off the ships. They would come ashore and wanted to go to what they called "geisha houses," which weren't geisha houses at all, but simply houses of prostitution. One of us would have to go along and interpret for them.

One case I remember involved three sailors who tried to break into a Japanese house—a house they mistakenly thought was a house of prostitution. It was actually occupied by a woman and her two children. The children followed the three sailors after they left until they found an MP, who then arrested them. They were then sent back to their ship. The sailors were tried on the ship, and the woman and her two children, plus a neighbor woman who helped identify the sailors, were summoned as witnesses. So for several days I had to accompany them out to the ship during the course of the trial, which had become somewhat of a contest between two of the officers, one posing as the prosecution and the other as defense counsel.

There was a great debate at the outset as to whether these Japanese could be sworn in as witnesses because they couldn't take an oath on the Bible. After considerable discussion, I was allowed to give them a statement about the importance of telling the truth, and the trial proceeded. It took several days, and I think at least two of the sailors were convicted, but I don't know what punishment was accorded to them.

I think I was in Japan for about six months when I had enough points to come home for discharge from the service. I went back to graduate school at Harvard in the beginning of 1948. My field of study in graduate school was government. There were only a couple of classes in the Government Department that dealt with Asia. I was well acquainted with several members of John Fairbank's first China study group, which included such figures as Benjamin Schwartz, Rhodes Murphy, Conrad Brant, and Marius Jansen, all of whom became scholars in the China field. My dissertation was entitled "The Role of the Japanese in Southeast Asian Nationalist Movements" and involved the effect of the Japanese occupation of various Southeast Asian countries on the development of nationalism in those countries.

I used some Japanese-language material, but I drew a good deal of material from documents that came out of the Tokyo war crimes trials. After I completed all of my work for the Ph.D., I placed my name at the Harvard Placement Office. Ohio University at Athens, Ohio, was looking for a replacement for a man who had retired, and this was in the middle of the year. Over the telephone, I was hired. I came to the university and was the third man in a three-man department. The university enrollment was about four thousand, and the teaching load was fairly heavy. My general teaching area was in comparative government and international relations. But as the university grew, and as the department took on more and more members, it became possible to add courses in specialization. Eventually, I was able to offer courses in the government and politics of Japan, and some time later, the government and politics of China. I also offered seminar-type courses in the field of U.S. policy in Asia. My whole academic career was almost directly the outgrowth of my experience with the Japanese-language school in Boulder, Colorado, and my experiences in Japan, which resulted from it. Summing up, I would have to say that my chance encounter with Lt. Cmdr. Hindmarsh back in the fall of 1942 had a major influence on my career.

# Navy Weatherman

## DR. GAYLORD WHITLOCK

*Dr. Gaylord Whitlock was born in 1917, in Mt. Vernon, Illinois. He graduated from Southern Illinois Normal University with a bachelor's degree in chemistry and education in 1939. He then won a scholarship to Pennsylvania State University in agriculture and biological chemistry. He stayed on long enough to earn a Ph.D. before enlisting in the U.S. Navy in 1943. He is now retired from the University of California and lives next to a golf course in Green Valley, California.*

When I got my Ph.D. I had 32 job offers. There were very few Ph.D.s in biochemistry in those days. I chose a job that would defer me from the draft until after the birth of my first child. The baby was born in January 1943, and in June I went to Des Moines, Iowa, and applied for a navy commission. The navy told me that as soon as the papers came through I could be a chemistry teacher at the Naval Academy in Annapolis. I thought that would be pretty good duty, but interestingly enough the papers got lost. In the meantime, I received my draft notice and I was in a rush to get my navy commission. I just had to sign the final papers. The navy gave me instructions to go ahead and try to make the navy quota, and [they said] "If you don't make the navy quota, tell the army you have a commission in the navy." Well, I made the navy quota. I was an apprentice seaman for one day, discharged the next day on a "Special Service Discharge," and then commissioned as an ensign in the United States Naval Reserve. But I didn't have any orders, and that was in June 1943. My orders did not come until December 1943, and my orders were to report to the Naval Training School in Aerological Engineering at the

178

University of California at Los Angeles. Aerology is the navy's term for meteorology, and meteorology is "weather guessing."

I arrived in Los Angeles at my own expense on a train from Ames, Iowa, and made my way to Westwood Village. My instructions were to go to 644 Landfair Avenue at the El Cielito Apartments, which were being used as bachelor officers' quarters for some of the navy personnel enrolled in this training program. I went to the El Cielito apartment building and knocked on a door. A handsome gentleman answered the door. I told him, "I understand I might find a room here." "Well," he said, "We are allowed to have five people to an apartment. Can you cook?" I said, "Yes, I can cook. I'm a nutritionist." "Well, then you can have a room," he said.

There was no smog in the Los Angeles basin in those days. In fact, it was so cool there that the summer white naval uniform was never the uniform of the day. The only time I wore dress whites was to be best man in my best friend's wedding.

There were 150 people in my class and we were the eighth class to go through there. After the three-semester course at UCLA we received a professional degree in meteorology, which was equivalent to a master's degree in physics, because we were in the physics department. The courses were tough, but we had some fun. The navy officers' club at the Ambassador Hotel welcomed us on Saturday nights, and generally on Sundays there were invitations to the homes of Hollywood celebrities. I became friends with Bing Crosby and his family and met a lot of other people like that.

Graduation was on 14 August 1944, my wife's birthday and our wedding anniversary. Then I got orders to go to La Jolla, California, to oceanographic school. I studied under fabulous people there. One of the things we were working on was a formula by which we could take a picture of waves on a coastline from ten thousand feet and predict the depth of the water along that shoreline. That became very, very important later on for all of the invasions in the Pacific and Europe. Knowing the fetch, which is the distance over which the wind blows, and the strength of the wind, you can calculate the height of the waves. Putting this all together helped us to then develop the slope of that shoreline. If you could see in the aerial photo where the waves were breaking, then you could determine the depth along that shoreline. I never had to use this formula, but I helped to develop it over the six-week period I was there.

After La Jolla, I received orders to go to Fleet Weather Central in Kodiak, Alaska. I arrived there, I think, in October 1944. My duties there were as junior watch officer, finally working my way up to senior watch officer, and reanalysis officer. The reanalysis officer reanalyzes yesterday's weather in the light of today's weather. We had to draw weather maps every six hours. We were in charge of all the weather forecasting for all the ships at sea and all the aircraft from San Francisco to Hawaii north.

We had radio operators who would pick up weather data from other stations. They were fabulous guys. I had one radio operator who could put one earphone over one ear and another earphone on the other ear and take reports from two different stations at the same time and type their reports.

Ens. Gaylord Whitlock, originally trained as an "aerologist" by the navy, and then sent to Utah to train as a chemical warfare officer. Fortunately, the war ended before he had a chance to test his new skills.

Then there was the night I got shipwrecked. Kodiak Harbor is about fifteen miles deep and about fifteen miles across the mouth. Our base was set back in the harbor with the mountains in back of the base. Heat from the base caused the clouds to rise so that the ceiling was 1,000 feet to 1,600 feet higher than at the mouth of the harbor where we had a radio rangefinder on Woody Island, and that's where airplanes would home in. We would give them a cloud ceiling from where we were well inside the harbor, but sometimes they would break through the clouds six hundred feet below where we told them they would. They didn't like that. Well, we had a patrol boat, an old converted fishing vessel that wasn't very seaworthy after guns had been mounted fore and aft, as well as depth charge racks and all sorts of other stuff. Japanese submarines had been spotted in the area and they wanted to protect the base, so this vessel would sail back and forth across the mouth of the harbor and past Woody Island every hour, twenty-four hours a day. So I said, "Let's teach these men on the patrol boat how to take weather observations." On a Sunday night I went aboard this ship and went out with these fifteen sailors to teach some of the enlisted men how to make ceiling observations and launch a pilot balloon with a transmitter on it. It would give us temperature, wind velocity, wind direction, and atmospheric pressure. On the second day, we ran into a williwaw. A williwaw is a downslope wind that comes down off the Siberian and Alaskan land areas. These winds are very much like the chinooks in the Midwest or the Santa Ana winds in Southern California.

It was at night, the skipper was seasick, and some of the men were getting seasick too. However, their orders were to stay on station, no matter what. But the skipper ordered the ship into the lee of Woody Island to get some protection from the winds. We then got washed up on an uncharted reef. We didn't sink. The crest of a wave picked us up and sat us down on top of the reef. Some of the men thought, "Well, we are only a mile and a quarter offshore; we can swim ashore." The water was twenty-nine degrees and we lost ten men out of the sixteen. (I was the sixteenth.) They froze to death before they got ashore. The executive officer was one of them. He made it to the beach, but died there.

I swam back into my cabin to get a picture of my wife and daughter. Our rescue ship was a Coast Guard buoy tender. It was in port to put a lighted buoy on the reef we had just run aground on, but couldn't get out to do it that day because of the storm. But he did come out that night to rescue us.

I tied a rope around myself and was the last to be pulled off the ship. They didn't even know I was aboard because I wasn't on the manifest. I was the one who sent out the SOS signal with a light before we lost power, but I sent it out so fast the people on shore couldn't make out what I said, as I learned later.

I was frozen from my hips down from being in the water, but what I was really worried about was when a beautiful nurse rubbed me down with cocoa butter and I couldn't feel it. I also had ruptured eardrums from the force of fifteen-foot waves breaking over the ship and hitting us. I recovered partially from that and continued on with my duties.

In July 1945, I was ordered to chemical warfare training at Dugway

Proving Grounds in Utah. All of the chemical warfare officers in the navy had to be weather guessers, because if you were going to have a chemical warfare offensive you had to know which way the wind was blowing to make it effective. On 14 August 1945 (August 15 on the other side of the International Date Line), we got up at four in the morning to drive over the mountains to Dugway. When we got to the gate there was nobody there. When we went in, all the nurses were having a party. We didn't know it then, but it was V.J. Day. The war was over and we were given the rest of the day off.

We did finish our chemical warfare training, however, and we must have had a chemical warfare offensive planned from Adak Island in the Aleutians, coming down through the Kuril Islands at the end of the Aleutians and hitting Japan from that direction. We had all kinds of chemical weapons stored in Alaska and I have often wondered whatever happened to them.

My next set of orders after the chemical warfare school were to go to Fleet Weather Central, which had been moved from Kodiak to Adak Island. (Adak is farther down the Aleutian chain and closer to Japan.) I got my wife and daughter back to Buffalo, New York, and I was supposed to then fly on to Seattle—Sand Point Naval Air Station—but was bumped en route by a typewriter. Dean Acheson (secretary of state under Truman) was aboard the USS *Missouri* and needed this typewriter to finish up the surrender documents that were to be signed in Tokyo Bay. At least that is what I was told. So I was bumped by a typewriter and had to fly commercial to St. Louis, where I caught an army transport to Stockton, California.

I finally made it to Adak and was there for about two weeks when our whole unit was shipped back to Kodiak. I got back to Kodiak in October, I think it was, and I developed an ear infection. They didn't know what to do with me in Kodiak, so they sent me to Seattle, and Seattle said, "Where do you want to go from here? You can choose any hospital you want." I said, "Get me to the closest one to Buffalo, New York, where my wife is."

I was in Sampson Naval hospital in the Finger Lakes region of New York for six months, getting constant injections of penicillin in my rear to cure my ear. Finally, I had enough points to get out of the navy. I took a half bottle of Mercurochrome and put it in one ear, and half a bottle in the other ear, and cleared up the infection and got out. However, before I left the navy they said they wanted me to go to Boulder, Colorado, for language training. I was given the choice of Chinese, and probably would have ended up on Amoy Island off the coast of mainland China, or Russian and probably would have gone to Petropavlovsk in eastern Siberia. Russia was still an ally at that time. I said, "No, thank you. I think I'll just get out."

A yearlater, while working at Merck & Co. Inc., I asked their therapeutic institute there to make a culture of my ear problem. They found out I had a cold water fungus that I had picked up during the shipwreck in Alaska, and it was not sensitive to penicillin.

"On V.J. Day—the day the war ended—we had
thousands of people who just walked off the job."

# Master Rigger, Mare Island Naval Shipyard

## CMDR. EDDIE MARTINEZ, USNR (RET.)

*Cmdr. Martinez was born in Vallejo, California, in 1911, a fifth-genera-
tion Californian. In 1928, at the age of seventeen, he started to work at
Mare Island Naval Shipyard in Vallejo, California, as an apprentice rigger, working his way up to master rigger and department head by the age
of 32. He retired from that job 43 years later, in 1971. In 1942 he enlisted
in the U.S. Naval Reserves. Because of his skills as a master rigger and supervisor, he was never called to active duty during World War II. However,
he was called to active duty during the Korean War and retired from the
Naval Reserves as a commander in 1971, the same year he retired from Mare
Island. Martinez is a very active ninety-year-old and still lives in Vallejo,
the city of his birth.*

My first ancestor to come to California was Don Ygnacio Martínez.
He was a cadet in the Spanish army in 1799, and ended up in California.
After Mexico won independence from Spain, he served the Mexican government. In those days they didn't have pensions and Social Security, so
they gave land grants to people instead. Don Ygnacio received this huge
Pinole land grant, part of which is now the town of Martinez, California. He then got involved in the political life of California, and became
the commandant of the Presidio in San Francisco and later the fourth
*alcalde,* or mayor, of San Francisco.

When I graduated from high school I had the intent of going on to college and becoming an engineer. I wanted to build bridges and sky-scrapers—all sorts of structural work—but because of the Depression I didn't have the money, so I took an apprentice exam at Mare Island and went to work as a rigger. I was fortunate enough to work my way up through the ranks to become a master rigger and shop supervisor. In those days, an apprentice made twenty-five cents an hour. I got a paycheck of $11.90 every week.

A lot of people ask me, "What does a rigger do?" Well, in the old days a rigger was somebody who rigged the sailing ships, the ropes that held the masts in place so that the sails could propel the ships, and if a ship wasn't rigged properly you could lose your masts and the ship would come to a stop. They used hemp rope in those days. That was in the age before steel ships and steel wires. I think steel wire started coming in around 1910. Of course, after the age of sail, the height of masts came down, and masts were used more for electronic equipment such as com-munications and radar. In the days of World War II, a rigger in the navy would be like a boatswain's mate—a deck type of rating.

William Shillingsburg was the master rigger when I started at Mare Island. He was also my mentor. For some reason I just felt that I wanted to be like him. When I started to work there at seventeen, Shillingsburg introduced me to Alonzo Gohlikey. He was an African-American Span-ish War veteran and my "apprentice counselor." He was really the first person at Mare Island to take me under his wing. When Shillingsburg introduced him to me, his words to Alonzo were something like this, "Take care of this kid, and see that he doesn't get hurt." Gohlikey said, "I got you, boss," or something like that. Alonzo must have been around fifty years old at that time and he remained a friend of mine for as long as he lived. He worked at Mare Island until he retired, which was in 1945, and lived to a ripe old age.

Another person who worked at Mare Island and who deserves men-tion is Edward Beutel. He was a World War I veteran and a chief quar-terman on the waterfront. He was one of my assistants after I became a master rigger and shop supervisor. He was a shaker and mover down on the waterfront at Mare Island. That's the only way I can describe him.

When I started to work as an apprentice rigger in 1928 we had forty-eight riggers in the shop. During the height of World War II, we had around 4,300 people, which was about ten percent of all the people working at the shipyard. Of those 4,300, 500 were actually classified as riggers. We had other people in our shop who weren't classified as riggers but were employed in other capacities, such as making cargo nets, embarkation nets, and radar antennas. We had salvage divers, small boat operators, crane operators, tank cleaners, and forklift operators. We were involved in the construction, launching, and repair of ships. Our shop ran three shifts a day, seven days a week, and was sort of like the Public Works Section of the Production Department at Mare Island.

I'm getting ahead of myself a bit, but in 1943, I was promoted to master rigger, and senior rigger supervisor of my shop at the age of thirty-two. I kept that position until I retired in 1971. In 1943, when I went into the Navy Reserve, I thought I would be called to active duty at least as a chief boatswain's mate, but the navy saw to it that I never got called to active duty. It wasn't until the Korean War that the navy made me an offer I couldn't refuse, and I served at the Yokosuka Naval Shipyard in Japan for sixteen months. My wife, Grace, was left pregnant and without a place to live. When I came home sixteen months later, she held up our new baby and said, "That's your daddy." During our forty-four years of marriage, Grace was always there, during good times and bad.

Even before Pearl Harbor, there was a sound in the distance. Things were happening. Somebody had bought three hundred buses and staged them at the south end of the shipyard. A dispatching center and a maintenance center were set up, and the buses were just sitting around like they were waiting for something to happen. And like I said, this was before 7 December 1941, maybe early 1941. Mare Island started hiring more people, and we started building more ships, mostly tenders—submarine tenders, destroyer tenders, and the like. Some of the ships that we launched in 1942 were well along in the construction phase in 1941, before Pearl Harbor.

We were also building submarines—fleet boats—and they, too, were under construction before Pearl Harbor. There were also ships coming in for routine maintenance and, after the war started, there were ships coming in for repairs from battle damage. Everything became well orchestrated. We were a very effective, efficient shipyard. We tried to make Mare Island hum like a Swiss watch. There was a real cooperation between the civilians and the military.

I guess you could say, like with any organization, we operated on a bell curve. We had the very good, the average, and the lesser types. But

I can't say enough good things about the apprentice programs we had at Mare Island. The old timers liked to pass on their knowledge to those who might replace them later on, and they took pride in their apprentices.

When I started the apprentice program when I was seventeen, it was a four-year program. Part of the time was spent in the shop and part of the time was spent going to school. We got a thorough education out of it. See, part of the apprentice program was to train future supervisors and administrators. So most of the supervisors, such as myself, were once apprentices.

On the morning of 7 December, I got a call from the duty officer at Mare Island, and he said there was an emergency meeting at the shipyard because Pearl Harbor had been bombed. When I asked him for more de-

**Cmdr. Eddie Martinez, a fifth-generation Californian, joined the U.S. Navy Reserves during World War II, but his work at Mare Island Naval Shipyard was so critical that he was not called to active duty during the war, but was later during the Korean War.**

tails, he told me to turn on the radio, and hung up. When I got to Mare Island, it was bedlam. I went to a conference, and the admiral in charge of the base said, "If the Japanese don't get through to the West Coast tonight or tomorrow morning they will never make it." So the first thing we started doing was to fill sandbags. Trucks full of sand came to Mare Island, and I don't know where the sandbags came from. That afternoon antiaircraft guns were brought in from the Benicia Arsenal and set up on the ball field at the north end of the island. We were trying to get ready in case the Japanese tried to invade. It was three days later before I went home to get some sleep.

After Pearl Harbor, the population of Vallejo grew from about 10,000 or 15,000 to over 40,000 at its peak. And one of the problems in

Vallejo during the war was housing. When those three hundred buses got rolling, they brought people from Sacramento to Mare Island, from San Jose to Mare Island, and from Santa Rosa to Mare Island, twenty-four hours a day, seven days a week, just taking people to and from work.

Of course, after the war started we got orders for new construction, but instead of routine maintenance on ships we were getting ships in for repair of battle damage. I remember the USS *Shaw*. We put a new bow on her. We built it before she arrived from Pearl Harbor. We put it in the dry dock, and the ship was brought in. We cut off the old bow—what was left of it—then floated the new one up and welded it on.

In the military, all shipyards have the same departments and shops and they are numbered. So if you go to Portsmouth or Philadelphia Naval Shipyards and you want to go to the electric shop, it will be Shop 51, the riggers are in Shop 72, and so on. So no matter where you went, that was how you found the shop you were looking for, and that is how orders were written. We even started color-coding the hard hats that people wore. All the service trades had different-colored hard hats so that if you needed a shipfitter or an electrician, for example, you could pick them out by the color of their hard hats.

Hunters Point Naval Shipyard, near San Francisco, took bigger ships with battle damage, and Mare Island was always loaning them people to help them out. And it was very unpleasant when we had to go into ships that had battle damage if there were still human remains inside. Gases developed inside some of the compartments from decomposing bodies and it was very unpleasant. We had to wear oxygen breathing apparatuses when we went in, and it bothered some more than others. The ones who were bothered the most weren't made to go in. And it wasn't just our shop that had to go into those compartments and do this sort of thing. It was all shops.

In those days we weren't up to speed on safety. People didn't wear earplugs. That was for sissies, and people would get what they called "shipyard ears." They were hard of hearing. Protective clothing and masks to protect from silicosis weren't used, and we did have accidents at the yard. All accidents were spectacular. In a shipyard there are no little accidents. Things were dropped from cranes; we overturned cranes by trying to push our luck. We had a wooden stage in one of the dry docks collapse and all of the men on the stage were killed except for one. The survivor was a rigger. Accidents don't happen; they're caused. Much of it was from having inexperienced people working in the yard.

Before Pearl Harbor, we had a lot of fleet reserve people working at Mare Island. When you retire from the navy you go into the fleet reserve until you have a total of 30 years. And they were all well trained, experienced people. When the war started, all of these people, many of whom were supervisors, were called back to active duty. Then, as soon as we got a new batch of apprentices trained, the draft came along and took them into the military too. So we started training programs where we trained people in more specialized areas, sort of the shortest distance between two points. As an apprentice, you were pretty well rounded. By training people to do specific tasks we could turn them out faster, but they were limited in what they could do. Some worked only on the inside of ships, some only on the outside. Some worked only on submarines. But even then, as soon as we got them trained, they were drafted. We had recruiters for the shipyard going all over the United States—Florida, South Carolina, Kansas—looking for people to work at Mare Island. Some of these new people had never seen the ocean before, and a lot of them were women. We had women splicing half-inch wire, making nets, sewing leather, and even operating cranes.

Then, too, we had civilian workers coming through Mare Island en route to places like Hawaii. They would gather at Mare Island until they had enough people and ships to make up a convoy before sending them out. We didn't want these people just sitting around, so we put them to work until they were shipped out. There were so many people coming and going that our census was never the same from day to day.

We also had some suspicious characters come to work for us. I think some of them were criminals who came to work for the shipyard and hide. Every once in a while the FBI or Treasury Department people would come in and take people away in handcuffs.

On V.J. Day—the day the war ended—we had thousands of people who just walked off the job. A crane was pulling a forty-ton boiler out of a ship, and it was about three-quarters of the way out when the crane operator shut down the crane and left it hanging there. People didn't stop to check out, never said goodbye, and some never came back to collect their last paycheck. Thousands did that. Some of them even left their cars. The war was over!

# Selected Bibliography

## Books

Blair, Clay, Jr. *Silent Victory, The U.S. Submarine War Against Japan.* Annapolis: Naval Institute Press, 1975.

Brokaw, Tom. *The Greatest Generation Speaks.* New York: Random House, 1999.

Costello, John. *The Pacific War 1941–1945.* New York: William Morrow and Company, 1981.

Dunnigan, James F., and Albert A. Nofi. *The Pacific War Encyclopedia.* New York: Checkmark Books, 1998.

_____, and _____. *Victory at Sea, World War II in the Pacific.* New York: William Morrow and Company, 1995.

Homes, W.J. *Double-Edged Secrets: U.S. Naval Intelligence Operations in the Pacific During World War II.* Annapolis: Naval Institute Press, 1979.

Madsen, Daniele. *Forgotten Fleet: The Mothball Navy.* Annapolis: Naval Institute Press, 1999.

Morison, Samuel Eliot. *The Two Ocean War: A Short History of the United States Navy in the Second World War.* New York: Little, Brown and Company, 1963.

Prangle, Gordon W. *Miracle at Midway.* New York: Penguin Books, 1983.

Pisano, Dominick A. *To Fill the Skies with Pilots: The Civilian Pilot Training Program, 1939–1946.* Washington and London: Smithsonian Institution Press, 2001.

Veigele, William J. *Patrol Craft of World War II.* Santa Barbara: Astral Publishing Company, 1998.

Y'Blood, William T. *The Little Giants: U.S. Escort Carriers Against Japan.* Annapolis: Naval Institute Press, 1987.

## Articles

"Citizens in the Officer Corps: An Examination of the ROTC's Past and Present," by Midshipman Daniel H. Else, U.S Naval Reserve, NROTC Unit, University of Illinois, Champaign, Illinois. Annapolis, U.S. Naval Institute Proceedings, July 1973.

"The Naval Reserve Officer Training Corps," by Captain C.W. Nimitz, U.S. Navy. First written in 1928, when the author was serving as the director of the NROTC at the University of California at Berkeley.

Peterson, Bernard Wiley USMCR Ret., "The Oral Memoirs of Captain Bernard Wiley Peterson USMCR," The Oral History Archive, American Airpower Heritage Museum, Midland, Texas.

## Useful Web Pages

The American University: A World War II Retrospective: V-12—Lawrence E. Lucchetti, R. Dennis Pool, and Elizabeth "Smith" Rodes. http://www.american.edu/arubin/wwii/v-12.htm.

DANFS Online—Dictionary of American Fighting Ships—maintained by Andrew Toppan. http://www.hazegray.org/danfs.

Pacific Wrecks Database—maintained by Justin Taylan. http://www.pacificwrecks.org.

World War II U.S. Veterans Website—maintained by Dick and Dave Berry. http://ww2.vet.org/default.asp.

# Index

Abbot, Capt. Royal W. 164
Admiralty Islands, minesweeping in 124–5
African-Americans: at Mare Island Naval Shipyard 185; in U.S. Navy 117, 133–4
aircraft carriers built on oiler hulls 74
Alameda Naval Air Station 30, 33
*Aldebaran* 164
Aleutian Islands 182; *see also* Whitlock, oral history
*Allen M. Sumner* 123
Anderson, Ens. W.G. 166
Angaur Island, minesweeping at 127
Anuda (Cherry Island) 120
*Apache* 130
Apra Harbor *see* Guam
*Argonne* 98
*Arizona* 20, 21, 23; *see also* Langdell, oral history
Arquette, Lt. Cmdr. James 64; oral history of 46–53
*Astoria* 104, 106, 109
Atkeson, John C. 94
attack transports *see* Barden, oral history
Attu, 90; *see also* Pierce, oral history
*Australia* 110–11, 131
Australia 42; U.S. forces in 101–2

*Bailey see* Hogshead, oral history
Bailey, Captain 140, 142, 151
Baker, Lt. (jg) D.N. 67
Ballard, Robert 107
Barden, Lt. Kenneth, oral history of 132–38
Barnett, Cmdr. Bill, oral history of 108–13
"Bat Teams" 57
Beatty, Adm. Frank 95
Beightler, General 69

*Betelgeuse* 116
Blazier, Robert 82
*Blue* 103, 106
Bode, Captain 105
Boettcher, Quartermaster Frank 152
Boles, Warren 109
Bouganville 38–42, 83,85
Bracket, Bruce 31
Brant, Conrad 176
Bright, Mark 59
Brock, Sam 175
Brockmeyer, Homer 51, 61, 64
Bruce, Alfred 67
*Buck* 25, 26
Buck, Congressman Frank 115
Buckmaster, Captain 82
Buerkle, Cmdr. Elmer C. 112
Bureau of Naval Personnel 27
Butler, Ens. R.D. 165
Butterfield, Captain 133

*The Caine Mutiny see* Wouk, Ens. Herman
*California* 143
Callaghan, Admiral 110
*Canberra* 109; *see also* Gregory, oral history
Caplan, Captain 129
Caprise, Lieutenant (jg) 147, 149
Carbullido, Joaquin 159
Carl, Gen. Marion 45
Castro, Bobby 44
Cator, Benjamin F., oral history of 124–31
Cebu Island 86
Cecil, Capt. Charles P. 110–13
Chamorros *see* Guam
*Charles Carroll see* Barden, oral history
*Chaumont* 159

193

*Chenango see* Malinasky, oral history
Cherry Island (Anuda) 120
*Chester* 25, 26
*Chicago* 103, 105
Childers, Lloyd 81–2
Clark Field 66, 67, 87
Coe, Capt. Charles 44
*Coghlan* 90
*Columbia* 130
*Coral Sea* 25
Corl, Harry 81–2
Corsairs (F4U) fighters: as night fighters
  57; *see also* Langstaff, oral history; Peter-
  son, oral history
*Cowanesque* 129
Culion Island leper colony 148
Curtin, John 101

*Dale* 90
*Dashiell* 145
Decious, Lt. Cmdr. Warren, oral history of
  157–62
destroyer escorts *see* Meyer, oral history of
destroyer minesweepers—fast minesweep-
  ers *see* Cator, oral history; Drachnik,
  oral history
Drachnik, Capt. Joseph B, oral history of
  114–23
Dugway Proving Grounds 181–2
Durbin, Jim 175
Durham, A.H. "Bull" 50
Dutch Harbor 89–90, 93

Efate 84
Elder, Lt. Arthur C. *see* Isaacs, oral his-
  tory
Eleventh Airborne *see* paratroopers
Elsbree, Willard H., oral history of 171–77
El Toro Marine Corps Air Station 43, 45
*Enterprise* 52, 55, 56, 65, 79, 82, 84
Erskine, Commander 173
Esders, Wilhelm 81–2
*Essex* 56, 57, 62
*Evans* 168

Fifth Marine Division, Japanese-language
  officer with 173–4
Filipinos 117; guerrillas *see* Vraciu, oral
  history; on board U.S. Navy ships 117
First Marine Division 135
Ford Island 20, 81, 97
Fort Pierce—amphibious boat base 132–3
French Indochina 153
Fuchida, Mitsuo 20–4
*Fuller* 106

Gay, Ensign 81
Gohlikey, Alonzo 185
Grasscamp, pilot off *Hornet* 67
Gregory, Lt. Cmdr. Jesse, oral history of
  100–7
Guadalcanal 37–42, 76, 82, 85, 109, 111;
  *PC-476* at 166–7; scouting squadron
  "Ringbolt" at 30–3; *Zane* at 116–23
Guam 152; Chamorros on 158–9
Gulf of Alaska 28–9
Gunterman, Sonarman Joseph 123

Hague, Melvin 31
Hall, Tom 57, 58
Halsey, Admiral 110–11, 143
Hansen, Swede 111
Hanson, Bob 41
Harrington, John F., oral history of 139–
  52
Harrison, Lt. Cmdr. H.W. 55–6
Harvey, Bob 35
Hayler, Captain 28–9
*Helena* 108–13
*Helm* 104
Henderson Field 31, 39, 119, 120
*Henrico* 136
Hickem Field 19, 20
*Hidalgo* 152
High-speed destroyer transports *see*
  Meyer, oral history
Hill, Chief Boatswain E.J. 22
Hindmarsh, Lieutenant Commander
  171–2, 177
*Hogan* 126
Hogshead, Stanley M., oral history of
  89–95
Hole, Lieutenant Commander (Australian
  Navy) 104
Hollandia 48, 59; minesweeping at 126
Holloway, Jim 116
Hong Kong 44
*Honolulu* 25, 28–9, 109
Hoover, Capt. Gilbert C. 110
*Hornet* 61, 81
*Hovey* 130
*Hugh P. Hadley* 168
Humbolt Harbor—New Guinea, mine-
  sweeping at 126
Hyde, Lt. (jg) Austin 151

*Idaho* 149
Ie Shima 135
*Independence* 55, 56
*Indianapolis* 136; rescue of survivors by
  *Ringness* 169–70
*Ingersol* 60

*Intrepid* 57–9
Iron Bottom Sound 107
Irons, Lieutenant Commander 30
Isaacs, Bernard, oral history of 153–6

Japanese-language officers *see* Elsbree, oral
history
Japanese-language school, Boulder, Colorado *see* Elsbree, oral history
Jensen, Marius 176
Jett, Commander 84
JICPOA—Joint Intelligence Center Pacific
Ocean Areas 173
Johnson, Osa 116
Johnstone, Midshipman (Australian Navy)
104
*Juneau* 110

Kahili (on Bouganville) 38–41
*Kaitens* 168
Kamikazes 129–31, 136, 143–4, 146
Karaberis, Lieutenant (later Admiral) 28
Katsura (instructor at Japanese-language
school, Boulder, Colorado) 172
*Kennison* 17
Kimmel, Admiral 17
King, Col. Howard 87–8
Kishimoto, Miss (instructor at Japanese-
language school, Boulder, Colorado)
172
Kiska 28–9, 90
Kodiak 29, 180, 182
Koener, Ozzie 111
Komandorski Islands, Battle of 90–3
Kossal Passage, minesweeping of 127
Kross, George 42
Kula Gulf, Battle of 109–13
Kwajalein 47, 57
Kyushu 87–8

*Laffey* 144
*Lamson* 145
Landing Signal Officer *see* Malinasky, oral
history
Lane, W.O. William J. 42
Langdell, Joseph K., oral history of 96–99
Langstaff, Lt. Col. H.A.P., oral history of
34–45
Larsen, Ens. Don 149, 152
*LCI (L)-981* 139–52
Leyte Gulf 145–9; landings at 142–3;
minesweeping at 128
*Liddle* 145
Lingayan Gulf 146; minesweeping at
128–9
Little, Lou 58

*Long* 124–31
*Long Island* 166
Los Negros Island 124
Loxton, Bruce (Australian Navy) 104–5
*LSM-318* 145
*LST-472* 146
*LST-738* 146
*Lurline* 85

MacArthur, General 67–8, 101–2; at Leyte
144–5; at Morotai 142
*Mahan* 145
Majuro 47, 60
*Makin Island* 65
Malaita 31
Malinasky, Cmdr. Frank, oral history 71–
77
Manus Island 124, 127–8, 131
*Marcus Island* 146
Marcus Island 55
Mare Island Naval Shipyard *see* Martinez,
oral history
"Marianas Turkey Shoot" (first battle of
the Philippine Sea) 50, 61–3
Marine Air Group Six 34, 43
Marine Corps fighter squadrons: VMF-
215 34–6, 45; VMF-223 85–8; VMF-
314 45; VMF-524 85
Martinez, Cmdr. Eddie, oral history of
184–9
*Maryland* 143
Massey, Cmdr. Lance 81
Mayo, Lt. (jg) Max 140
McCambell, Cmdr. David 62
*McCawley* 123
McMorris, R. Adm. Charles 90, 92
McVay, Capt. Charles B. 169–70
*Mervine* 131
Meyer, Capt. William C., oral history of
163–70
Midway Island 80–1
Miller, Cmdr. Norman "Bus" 154
Milli Atoll 48, 59
Mindanao 86
Mindoro Island 86, 145, 153–5
minesweeping *see* Cator, oral history
*Minneapolis* 30
*Mississippi* 143
Mitcher, Admiral 60
Mittnet, Ralph 158
Miyazaki 87
*Moale* 146
*Monaghan* 90
*Monterey* 52, 164
Moratai, landings at 142
Mortz, Chief 83

*Mt. Hood* 128
Mt. Pinatubo 66
Munda 38, 42–3, 122
Munger, Cmdr. Malcolm 94
Murphy, Rhodes 176
"Mustanger" 137; *see also* Decious, oral
  history

Nagomo, Admiral 23
*Nashville* 142, 145
Nasugbu—Philippines 147
*National Geographic* 116
*Nautilus* 167
Naval Academy 15, 25, 26, 89, 108, 114–
  16
Naval Air Groups: Nineteen 66; Six 59;
  Three 81; Twenty 66, 69
Naval reserve programs: NROTC *see*
  Meyer, oral history; V-5 85; V-12 132
Navy "Aerology" *see* Whitlock, oral his-
  tory
Navy Bombing Squadron Six 55
Navy Cross 22, 23, 94
Navy fighter squadrons VF-3 55; VF-6
  55, 57; VF-16 46–7, 62–4; VF-17 42;
  VF-20 66–7; VF-36 25
Navy floatplanes: OS2U 28; SOC3 30; *see
  also* Pierce, oral history
Navy patrol squadron (VP-43) 27
Navy torpedo squadrons: Five 81; Six 55
Ndume Island 122
Neefus, Jim 36–7, 41
Neff, Ziggie 63
Negros Island 86
*Nevada* 15–24
*New York* 96
*Newman* 168
*Newman K. Perry* 95
Nimitz, Cmdr. Chester: as admiral 170; as
  commanding officer NROTC at U.C.
  Berkeley 164
Nimitz, Chester, Jr. 164
*North Carolina* 109
Northwestern University 96, 165

O'Brian 144
O'Hare, Butch 55–7
Okinawa 87–8; Buckner Bay 150
*Oklahoma* 21
Oldendorf, Adm. Jesse 143
Oliver, Able Seaman (Australian Navy)
  104–5
Operation Magic Carpet 136
*Oriskany* 25

Palau 48, 59

Palawan Island, massacre of American
  POWs on 147–8
Panay Island 86
paratroopers, 186th 147
patrol craft: *PC-476* 165–6; *PC-477* 166;
  *PC-479* 166
*Patterson* 103–6
Pearl Harbor 15, 17–24, 27–8, 37, 46–8,
  66, 69, 79, 80–1, 94, 108–9, 116, 136,
  165; JICPOA at 173
Peleliu 86, 94; minesweeping at 127
*Pennsylvania* 23
Pensacola 25–6, 72
*Perry* 127
Perry, H.A. 87
Peterson, Capt. Bernard W., oral history of
  78–88
Peterson, Ensign 149
Phillips, Lieutenant Commander 56–7
Pierce, Capt. Larry, oral history of 25–
  33
Polk, Lt. (jg) George 32–3
Polk, Johnnie 159
Polk Awards *see* Polk, Lt. (jg) George
*Portland* 82, 122, 147
Post, Vic 111
POWs 38, 44–5; Australian 101; in Ger-
  many 155; *see also* Palawan Island
*President Hoover* 26
*Puget Sound* 34, 43–4
Puget Sound Naval Shipyard 26
Punch Bowl Cemetery 99
Pyle, Ernie, aboard *Charles Carroll* 135

*Quincy* 104, 106, 109
Quonset Point 46

Rabaul 42, 55
*Radford* 111, 113
*Ralph Talbot* 103
*Ranger* 72–3
Recial, Leonard 31
*Refuge* 160
*Register* 169
Reinhardt, "Chief" Lou 36
Richardson, Admiral 17
*Richmond* 16
*Ringness* 168–70
Rivers, J.G. 165
Robertson, Arvon J. 18
Royal Hong Kong Volunteer Corps 44
Russell Islands 31, 85, 121–2

*Sable* 77
St. *Louis* 109, 113, 123
St. *Paul* 150

Saipan 60, 94; minesweeping at 126; UDT at 126, 152
*Salt Lake City* 90–2
*San Francisco* 109–10
Sanderson, Neil (Australian Navy) 104
*Saratoga* 79–84
Sasavele 122–3
Savo Island, Battle of 118; *see also* Gregory, oral history
Scanland, Capt. F.W. 22
Schwartz, Benjamin 176
Scott, Admiral 110
Scott, Lieutenant (jg) 152
Scouting Squadron "Ringbolt" 25–33
Sealark Channel 119
Seeadler Channel 124–5
*Seminole* 120
Shanghai 150–1
*Shaw* 188
Shillingsburg, William 185
Shinohara's (Guam) 158
Shively, Signalman Wilber 149
*Shropshire* 102
*Stanly* 145
Steele, Commander 173
Stockton, Major 67
Strauss, Capt. Elliot 133
Struble, R. Adm. A.D. 144–5
Surigau, Strait 128; Battle of 143

*Talbot* 122, 146
Tanaka, R. Adm. Raizo 166–7
Tanapag Harbor 60
Tarawa 47, 56, 76, 94
Task Force 58, 49, 64
Tassafaranga, Battle of 30
Taussig, Joe 19
*Tennessee* 143
*Teruzuki* 166
Thieme, Robert 168
Thomas, R. Adm. Francis, oral history of 15–24
Thwing, Commander 133
Tinian 60, 94; minesweeping at 126–7
Tokyo Bay 43
"Tokyo Express" 30
Tomes, Major 38–41
Tongatabu 84

*Trevor* 119
Truck Island 57–9
Tulagi 3–3; *PC-476* at 165–7; *Zane* at 119–22
Turner, Admiral 121, 123

Ulithi 47, 66, 69, 169
*Underhill* 170

Vacaville High School 114–5
Vallejo 29; *see also* Martinez, oral history
*Valley Forge* 159
Vance, Ens. J.W. 102
*Vancennes* 104, 106, 109
Veazey, Lieutenant Commander 60
Vella Lavella Island, *Helena* survivors on 113
Vraciu, Cmdr. Alexander 48, 49, 50, 51; oral history of 54–70

Wake Island 47, 55, 79–80
Walne, Mrs. Florence 172
*Ward* 145
*Wasp* 47, 82, 109
*West Virginia* 143
Whangpoo River 150–1
White Russians 150
Whitlock, Dr. Gaylord, oral history of 178–183
Widhelm, Gus 60
Wilber, Ens. D.P. 165
Wiley, Delmar 82–3
Williams, Herb 41
*Wilson* 104
Wirtz, Lt. Cmdr. Peyton L. 117
Woleai 48
*Wolverine* 79
Wood, Major General 31
Wouk, Ens. Herman 123
Wright, R. Adm. Carlton 30

Yokusuka 44
*Yorktown* 81–2

*Zane* 116–23
*Zeilin* 116
Zumwalt, Elmo 116